Saint Paul in Britain

Christianity in Roman Britain – the Ancient Apostolic Foundations of the Church

By R. W. Morgan

Published by Pantianos Classics

ISBN-13: 978-1-78987-294-1

First published in 1860

Contents

Dedication iv

Preface v

Chapter One 6

Chapter Two - Historic Positions of Britain and the Roman Empire at the Commencement of the Christian Era 19

Chapter Three - The British Royal Family at Rome. — The Arimathaean, or First Introduction of Christianity into Britain . 38

    "Ad Britannos veni post Christum Sepelivi. Docui. Quievi." 48

    Nero 56

Chapter Four – The Tracings of the Ancient Royal Church of Britain to its Apostolic Foundations 64

    Triads of Paul the Apostle 77

Conclusion 82

Dedication

To Connop, Lord Bishop of St. David's representative and successor, in the primitive metropolitan see of Britain, of the national saint of the Cymry.

The following pages, a slight homage to his varied and profound accomplishments as a scholar, his Catholicity of spirit as a Christian, and his conscientious mastery, as a bishop of souls, of the language of his people, are, by permission, dedicated, by his very faithful servant,

R. W. Morgan.

Preface

A faithful account of the origin of native British Christianity as opposed to the Papal system first introduced four hundred and fifty-six years subsequently by Augustine the monk, is here, in readable compass, presented to the public. The history of such origin is inseparably blended with the long-sustained resistance of our early forefathers to the invasions of their liberties by the greatest empire of antiquity, wielding against them the military forces of nearly three-quarters of the globe. The events thus recorded have left their moulding power to this day on our constitution in Church and State. The most cursory glance at them is sufficient to demonstrate the untenableness of the supposition that Britain is indebted to Germany — a country which has never itself been free — for its free institutions, or to Italy for its Gospel faith. The leading principles of her laws and liberties are of pure indigenous growth; and her evangelical faith was received by her directly from Jerusalem and the East, from the lips of the first disciples themselves of Christ. The struggles in after ages down to our own period for the restoration and preservation of these indigenous birthright liberties, this primitive apostolical faith, constitute the most stirring and ennobling portions of our annals; and we may rest assured that as long as in their modern developments of British Protestantism, British Patriotism, and British Loyalty, they continue to inspire the national heart, our island will continue to retain her position in the vanward of the march of Order, Liberty, and Progress.

Dec. 24, 1860.

Chapter One

Westward of Italy, embracing Hispania, Gallia, the Rhenish frontiers, portions of Germany and Scandinavia, with its headquarters and great seats of learning fixed in Britain, extended the Druidic religion. There can be no question that this was the primitive religion of mankind, covering at one period in various forms the whole surface of the ancient world.

The ramifications of Druidism penetrated, indeed, into Italy, Greece, and Asia Minor; nor did Plato hesitate to affirm that all the streams of Greek philosophy were to be traced, not to Egypt, but to the fountains of the West. The pre-historic poets of Greece anterior to the mythologic creations of Homer and Hesiod, were, as their names imply, Druids — Musasus, Orpheus, Linus, (knowledge, the harp, the white-robed). Such historians were necessarily poets, for with the Druids metre was the vehicle of instruction. The visit of the British Druid, Abaris, was long remembered at Athens. Greek fancy converted the magnetic needle by which he guided his travels into an arrow of Apollo which would transport him at wish whithersoever he pleased. A more celebrated Druid, Pythagoras, founded a school in Italy the effects of which, though he himself and many of his leading scholars perished in a popular commotion, were never wholly obliterated; the transmigration of souls, their preexistence and immortality, the true theories of the heavenly bodies and their revolutions, the severity of the esoteric system with its silence and secrecy, being observed by various Italian sects down to the Christian era. In the Aegean Sea, Samothrace and Delos were Eastern cells of the same priesthood, the same rites being observed as in Britain, and embassies at stated periods exchanging visitations. [1] In earlier ages the City of Circles in Asia Minor — Troia (Troy) — and the Minoan Labyrinth in Crete were seats of the same widely-extended religion, and in Egypt the name of the great mother-temple, Carnac, identifies its remote founders with those of the mother-temple of the same name in Bretagne, both meaning 'the high stones of worship.' In the East, however, the principles of Druidism could only be traced in its earliest records, whilst on the continent of Europe they bore in practice and development the same corrupt relation to primitive Druidism as at present the Roman Catholic religion in the same countries does to primitive Christianity. In Britain, on the contrary, it had, for many reasons — the inaccessibility of the island, its freedom from foreign invasion, its character of sanctity, its possession by Gomeridae — retained in great degree its original purity. In the time of St. Paul it had been for a period of two thousand years the established religion; and the attachment of the people to its rule, with the desperate and well-sustained defence they made in its behalf and that of their country against the whole force of the Roman Empire in the meridian of its power, confirm the impression left by a dispassionate examination of the remains of its theology which have descended to us in the ancient British tongue, namely, that it was a highly moral, elevating, and beneficent religion, a superstructure not unworthy the principle on which it assumed to be built, and by which it offered itself to be judged, "The truth against the world," (*Y Gwir erbyn y Byd*).

It has been observed by the historian Hume, "that no religion has ever swayed the minds of men like the Druidic." The determined efforts of the Roman empire to overthrow its supremacy, and, if possible, suppress it altogether, prove that its rulers had been made practically aware of this fact. A Druidic triad familiar to the Greeks and Romans was, "Three duties of every man: Worship God; be just to all men; die for your country [2]." It was this last duty, impressed by a thousand examples and precepts, and not its religious tenets or philosophy, which caused Druidism to be marked for destruction by an empire which aspired to universal dominion and to merge all nationalities in one city. The edicts of the Emperors Augustus and Tiberius proscribed it throughout their dominions, making the exercise of the functions of a Druidic priest, as those of the Roman priest in the reigns of the Tudor sovereigns in England, a treasonable offence. But nations cannot be proscribed. The Druidic colleges in Britain, the only free state in Europe at this period, continued to educate and send forth their alumni to all parts of the Continent. Not till A.D. 43, that is, fourteen years only before the arrival of St. Paul in Rome, did the second, or Claudian invasion of Britain take place. It took ten years of incessant warfare to establish a firm footing in the south of the island; nor was it till seven years after the fall of Caractacus that the Roman state ventured to give its legions orders to carry out the leading object of the invasion — the destruction by force of arms of the Druidic cori, or seminaries, in Britain. The Boadicean war and the death of 80,000 Roman citizens were the first results of this policy of religious "dragonnades."

Summary of Druidic Theology

Druidism was founded by Gwyddon Ganhebon, supposed to be the Seth of the Mosaic genealogy, in Asia, in the year when the equinox occurred in the first point of Taurus, or the constellation of the Bull. Every year the equinoctial year is completed about twenty minutes before the sun has made a complete revolution from a certain star to the same star again. This arises from the precession of the equinoxes, or from a slow revolution of the pole of the equator round that of the ecliptic. In 25,920 years the pole of the equator makes one entire revolution round that of the ecliptic: hence the equinoctial colure occurs before it did the preceding year. In 72 years the precession amounts to one degree. If therefore, we have the equinoctial or solstitial point given in the ecliptic at any unknown period, it is easy to discover, by comparing it with the present solstitial point, how long that period is past. When the Druidic system was founded, the equinox, on the 1st of May, occurred in the first point of Taurus, which first point is now, on the 1st of May, 80 degrees from this solstitial point. It requires 72 years to recede one degree. Eighty degrees multiplied by 72 gives 5,760, the exact date when Druidism commenced, i.e., 3,903 years before the Christian era, 181 years after the creation of man, and 50 years after the birth of Seth. The astral bull of milk-white hue, its horns crowned with golden stars, became the symbol, or visible sacrament, of Druidism. In process of time the symbol, as usual, superseded in the East the thing signified, and Druidism became that tauric religion which gave the Crimea the appellation of the Tauric Chersonese. Extending thence, this corruption became the religion of Mithras in Persia, of Baal in Assyria, of Brahma in India, of Astarte or the Dea Syria in Syria, of Apis in Egypt, and in later ages, transferred from Egypt, of the two "Apis" (or calves as they are rendered in our version of the Scriptures) of the kingdom of Israel. [3] In all these religions the bull, or Taurus, was the sacred animal, and the symbol was preserved free, as far as we can judge, from idolatry by the Gomeridae of Britain. The bull was the sign and representant of the great Druidic isle, and the name still, in common parlance, continues to indicate a Briton of Britain as distinguished from the rest of the world.

From Asia Druidism was brought into Britain by Hu Gadarn, or the Mighty, its first colonizer, a contemporary of the Patriarch Abraham, and under his successors, Plennydd, Goron, Alawn, and Rhivon, it assumed its complete organization, becoming both the ecclesiastical and civil constitution of the island. About five centuries before the Christian era, its civil laws were codified by Dunwal Moelmud, the British Numa, and have since that period remained the common, unwritten, or native laws of the island, as distinguished from the Roman, the canon, and other codes of foreign introduction. These British or Druidic laws have been always justly regarded as the foundation and bulwark of British liberties. [4] The examination of them does not fall within our present purpose. The civil code and the sciences were taught by the Druids — orally or in writing indifferently — to every citizen, but the Druidic system of divinity was never committed to writing, nor imparted except to the initiated, and then under obligations to secrecy of a very awful character. It is, however, to the infraction of these obligations, when their force had been impaired by the influences of Christianity, that we are indebted for such knowledge as we possess of the real principles of the primitive religion of our island. Druidism taught as follows: —

The universe is infinite, being the body of the being who out of himself evolved or created it, and now pervades and rules it, as the mind of man does his body. The essence of this being is pure, mental light, and therefore he is called Du-w, Duw (the one without any darkness). His real name is an ineffable mystery, and so also is his nature. [5] To the human mind, though not in himself, he necessarily represents a triple aspect in relation to the past, present, and future; the creator as to the past, the saviour or conserver as to" the present, the renovator or re-creator as to the future. In the re-creator the idea of the destroyer was also involved. This was the Druidic trinity, the three aspects of which were known as Beli, Taran, Esu or Yesu. When Christianity preached Jesus as God, it preached the most familiar name of its own deity to Druidism; and in the ancient British tongue 'Jesus' has never assumed its Greek, Latin, or Hebrew form, but remains the pure Druidic 'Yesu.' It is singular thus that the ancient Briton has never changed the name of the God he and his forefathers worshipped, nor has ever worshipped but one God. [6]

The symbol of the ineffable name of the Deity were three rays or glories of light. Every Druid bore these in gold on the front of his mitre.

Other names of the deity were Deon, Dovydd, Celi, Tor, Perydd, Sol, Rhun, Ner.

In the infinite Deity exist in some incomprehensible mode, indivisible from himself, infinite germs, seeds, or atoms (*manred, manredit*), each in itself full and perfect deity, possessing the power of infinite creativeness. This branch of Druidic theism is involved in profound obscurity. It appears to have supplied Democritus with his theory of the atomic powers of nature, and Plato with his typal forms in the mind of the Deity. Matter was created and systematized simultaneously by the Creator's pronouncing His own name. It cannot exist without God. Nature is the action of God through the medium of matter. The laws of nature are, in the strictest sense, the laws of God, and that which is a violation of the laws of nature is necessarily a violation of the laws of God. [7]

The universe is in substance eternal and imperishable, but in form it is subject to successive cycles of dissolution and renovation. There is no such thing as annihilation in matter. Every particle of matter is capable of all forms of matter, and each form has its own laws of existence and action.

Around every separate existence, wherever it be, extends infinity; this is 'Ceugant' (the infinite space, or all-of-being, ubiquity), which God alone can fill, sustain, or uphold.

There were originally but two states of sentient existence — God in 'Ceugant,' and the 'Gwynfydolion' (the beings of the happy, literally 'white' state) in 'Gwynfyd.' The only aberration to which the 'Gwynfydolion' were liable was 'balchder.' 'Balchder' consisted in trying to do that which God only can do, enter and sustain 'ceugant,' uphold and govern the infinite universe. Certain of the 'Gwynfydolion,' whose numbers are known only to God, attempted to do so, and thus originated in themselves the state of 'Annwn.' 'Annwn' is the lowest possible point of conscious existence, in which the evil is wholly unmitigated by any particle of good. This result was the inevitable consequence of their act itself, not an external penalty imposed by God. To restore them to the state of 'gwynfyd,' God in His goodness created the third state of 'Abred.' 'Abred' includes all conditions of sentient life under 'gwynfyd.' Its lowest point is 'annwn;' its highest that immediately next to that of the 'Gwynfydolion,' the state of man, humanity. All 'abred' under humanity was termed 'byd maur,' the great 'byd.' Humanity itself was termed 'byd bychan,' the little 'byd' (world), because as all the infinite was contained in God, so all the cycles of existence below man were contained and represented in man. [8]

'Abred' is a state of probation and suffering for the 'Abredolion,' that is, for the 'Gwynfydolion' in 'abred' the reason being that, moral liberty of choice and action, or willinghood, being the essence of 'gwynfydiaeth,' or the spirit-life, there is nothing *per se* to prevent the 'Gwynfydolion' when they shall have re-attained heaven, from committing 'balchder' a second time, and thus reincurring its consequences. God created 'abred' to be a state of suffering, that in the vivid recollection of its pains and degradations the 'Gwynfydolion' might possess in themselves the surest moral guarantee against a repetition of their folly. 'Abred' was, therefore, essentially the creation of God's mercy, and its sufferings were indispensable to fulfil the object of such mercy towards the fallen beings for whom it had been so created. [9]

In the 'byd mawr' below man there was no responsibility, for there was no liberty of choice. Responsibility began with the 'byd bychan' or manstate, because there began such liberty. Hence the essence of the soul, according to the Druids, was the will, and the essence of religion was willinghood. Without freedom of will there was no 'humanity' in its distinguishing sense from animal life, nor any life or light in the soul which continued marw, void of living action and imbruted. Freedom of conscience was both the birth and breath of manhood, without which it was not manhood at all, but brutality — the soul resembling foetus undeveloped in the womb.

Reason appears to have been regarded by the Druids as a faculty common to all sensitive creatures, the difference in their physical organization being the cause of the difference in its degrees.

Mankind are the fallen 'Gwynfydolion.' Every human being has been in the angelic state in heaven ('gwynfyd'), fell thence to 'annwn,' rose thence through the various cycles of 'abred' probationary existence to his present state ('byd bychan'), in which he is again a free agent, master of his own spiritual destinies. If his soul willingly prefers good and abides by its choice, then at the dissolution of the body it re-enters 'gwynfyd,' from which it fell. This is the restoration. If his soul prefers evil, it again lapses back to some cycle in 'abred' best calculated to purify it from it. For 'abred' is the cycle of purification by suffering. 'Balchder' alone plunged the soul back to the lowest point, 'annwn,' and of this man could not be guilty; hence the proverb, "But once in 'annwn.'" Inhumanity sunk the soul to the condition nearest 'annwn.'

In the 'byd mawr,' below man, evil and suffering preponderate. In the 'byd bychan,' or 'man-state,' good and evil are equipoised. With 'byd bychan' probation terminates. In 'gwynfyd' pure good and pure happiness commence.

A soul might relapse countless times from 'byd bychan' back to 'abred,' and again rise. Ultimately every soul would pass 'byd bychan'; and when the last of the 'Gwynfydolion' had regained 'gwynfyd,' then would be the end of 'abred' ('terfyn abred') [10], the purpose for which it had been created being fulfilled. 'Abred' being dissolved, there would remain only the two states which existed from the beginning, 'Ceugant' and 'Gwynfyd.' According to the Druidic system, the 'hell' of man was past before his birth, and hell itself was a temporary state. 'Gwynfyd' was re-attainable through 'abred' only and its conditions, 'abred' through 'annwn' only and its conditions. 'Annwn' and 'abred' were the pre-conditions of the re-attainment of 'gwynfyd.' The knowledge and suffering of evil was held the *sine quâ non* to the understanding and appreciation of good, being the only means whereby their difference could be realized to ourselves. Suffering was regarded as the pre-essential of enjoyment.

The faculty of the soul which constituted more especially its eternity, or imperishable self-identity, is cov, or memory. The memory of all the evils and existences it has undergone in 'abred' forms or develops in the soul immediately it re-enters 'gwynfyd,' and not before. For the end of such memory is to preserve such 'Gwynfydolion' from a second fall. In the 'abred' cycles there is a suspension of 'cov,' and of the consciousness of self-identity.

The doctrine of transmigration was certainly Druidic, but it is equally certain that it was held by the Druids in a sense the Greek and Italian schools of philosophy have failed to transmit to us. The following extract the *Coelbren Rhodd,* [11] obscure as it is, may cast some light on the subject: —

"*Master.* What art thou?
"*Disciple.* A man.
"*M.* How?
"*D.* By the will of God. What God wills must be.
"*M.* Why art thou not something else than man?
"*D.* What God wills cannot be otherwise.
"*M.* Where art thou?
"*D.* In 'byd bychan.'
"*M.* Whence art thou come?
"*D.* From 'byd mawr.'
"*M.* What wert thou doing in 'byd mawr'?
"*D.* Traversing the cycle of 'abred.'
"*M.* Where wert thou before thou didst begin to traverse 'cylch abred'?
"*D.* In 'annwn.' "*M.* What wert thou in 'annwn'?
"*D.* The least of life that could be in itself, the nearest to the teeth of the dead. And in all forms and through all forms that are called body and life am I come hither into 'byd bychan' and misery and trouble have been my condition for ages and ages since I was delivered from 'annwn' and separated therefrom through the hand of God and His love, endless and indestructible.

"*M.* Through how many 'rhith' (forms of life) art thou come, and what has been thy 'damwain' (character of life)?

"*D.* Through every 'rhith' that can possess or be called life-in-itself, and my 'damwain' has been all misery, all hardship, all evil, all suffering, and little of good or happiness has there been of me before I am man.

"*M.* Through the love of God thou sayest thou art come through all this and hast felt all this — how so, seeing there are so many signs of unlove?

"*D.* 'Gwynfyd' cannot be regained without knowing everything, there cannot be knowing everything without feeling-in-self everything, there cannot be feeling everything without suffering-in-self every 'rhith' of evil and of good, that one may be self-known from the other; and all this must be before 'gwynfyd' can be regained, for 'gwynfyd' is perfect liberty, choosing the good when all forms of good and evil have been self-suffered.

"*M.* Why cannot there be 'gwynfyd' without traversing every 'rhith' of life in 'abred'?

"D. Because no two 'rhiths' are identical, and every 'rhith' has its own cause, suffering, means of knowledge, intelligence, 'gwynfyd,' power, not to be found in any other 'rhith'; and since there is special knowledge in every special 'rhith' not to be found in any other, necessity ensues to suffer every 'rhith' before 'abred' be completely traversed.

"M. How many 'rhiths' are there?

"D. As many as God saw necessary towards knowing all good and all evil in every kind and quality, so that there should be nothing conceivable by God which should not be experienced, and thence its 'abred' - knowledge." — (Coelbren Rhodd, p. 1.)

The happiness of 'gwynfyd' consisted in 'nevoedd,' i.e. eternal progressions of new scenes with new faculties of happiness. Herein, as in its notion of the time and object of "hell," Druidism differed from Christianity, which represents heaven as an eternal sabbath or rest. [12]

A soul that had passed 'byd bychan' might resume the morphosis of humanity for the good of mankind. The re-incarnation of such was always a blessing.

The lapse of a soul in 'byd bychan' began at the moment when it voluntarily preferred vice to virtue, for the will is its essence.

A new form of life, or the entrance into another cycle of existence, [13] ensued simultaneously with death.

Man had the power by accepting every evil as his part of 'abred' (or purification for 'gwynfyd'), to turn it to good. Hence willing suffering for our own good or that of others was the test-virtue of humanity, or 'byd bychan.'

Every soul guilty of crime, by voluntarily confessing it and embracing the penalty prescribed, expiated its guilt, and if in other respects good, re-entered 'gwynfyd.'

Except by the laying down life for life there could be no expiation or atonement for certain kinds of guilt. Caesar's words on this point are remarkable: — "The Druids teach that by no other way than the ransoming of man's life by the life of man, is reconciliation with the divine justice of the immortal gods possible." — (Comment., lib. v.) The doctrine of vicarious atonement could not be expressed in clearer terms.

The value of an atonement, or expiatory sacrifice, was in proportion to the value of the life sacrificed.

In all the changes of the 'byd mawr,' until it assumed the morphosis of man, the soul was in occultation, or eclipse.

The temples of the Druids were hypaethral, circular, and obelistic, i.e., open above and on every side, representing in form the dome of heaven, and composed of monoliths, or immense single stones, on which metal was not allowed to come. The dracontic, or circular form, symboled the eternal cycle of nature. The monolithic avenues leading to and from the temple, usually known as the dragon's head and dragon's tail, were in some instances seven miles long. The national religious processions moved through these on the three great festivals of the year.

All the prehistoric temples of Palestine, Persia, Italy, and Greece, commonly called Cyclopean or Pelasgic, were Druidic.

Stonehenge, the Gilgal of Britain, is the wreck of four thousand years' exposure to the elements. Its first founder was Hu Gadarn, B.C. c. 1800.

There were in Britain south of the Clyde and Forth forty Druidic universities, which were also the capitals of the forty tribes, the originals of our modern counties, which preserve for the most part the ancient tribal limits. Hence, for instance, Yorkshire retains the same disproportioned magnitude to our other counties as the territories of the Brigantes, its British tribe, did to those of the other tribes. Of these forty seats nine have disappeared, the remainder were as follows: —

Three seats of the three Arch-Druids of Britain. [14]

Caer Troia, or Caer Lud, or Caer Llyndain (the city of the lake of the Tain (Thames), or of the beautiful lake, tain meaning fair or beautiful, hence the Tain so called in British, Tyne still in North Britain), London.

Caer Evroc, York.

Caer Lleon, Caerleon.

Seats of the Chief Druids of Britain: —

Caer Caint, Canterbury.
Caer Wyn, Winchester.
Caer Werllan, afterwards *Caer Municipium,* St. Alban's, or Verulam.
Caer Salwg, Old Sarum.
Caer Grawnt, Cambridge, or Granta.
Caer Leil, Carlisle.
Caer Meini, Manchester.
Caer Gwrthegion, Palmcaster.
Caer Coel, Colchester.
Caer Gorangon, Worcester.
Caerlon ar Dwy, Chester.
Caer Peris, Porchester.
Caer Don, Doncaster.
Caer Guoric, Warwick.
Caer Meivod, Meivod.
Caer Odor, Bristol.
Caer Llyr, Leicester.
Caer Urnach, Uroxeter.
Caer Lleyn, Lincoln.
Caer Gloyw, Gloucester.
Caer Cei, Chichester.
Caer Ceri, Cirencester.

Caer Dwr, Dorchester.
Caer Merddin, Caermarthen.
Caer Seiont, Caernarvon.
Caer Wysc, Exeter.
Caer Segont, Silchester.
Caer Baddon, Bath.

The lapse of two thousand years has made but slight alteration in the names of these primitive cities of Britain. The Romans invariably fixed upon the chief caer of a British tribe, generally the strongest military position in its bounds, for their castra: hence the castra and Chester superseded the caer or British citadel; but the British name itself survived the Roman. Llyndain is still London, not Augusta; Werllan, Verulam, not Municipium; Caer Col, Colchester, not Camalodunum, &c, &c.

The students at these universities numbered at times sixty thousand souls, among whom were included the young nobility of Britain and Gaul. It required twenty years to master the circle of Druidic knowledge; nor, when we consider the great range of acquirements which the system included, can we wonder at the length of such probation. Natural philosophy, astronomy, arithmetic, geometry, jurisprudence, medicine, poetry, and oratory were all proposed and taught, the first two with severe exactitude. The system of astronomy inculcated had never varied, being the same as that taught by Pythagoras, now known as the Copernican or Newtonian. [15] The British words for 'star' 'astronomer' 'astronomy' are *seren, seronydd, seronyddiaeth;* hence the usual Greek term for the Druids was *Saronidoe,* astronomers. Of the attainments of the Druids in all the sciences, especially in this of astronomy, classic judges of eminence, Cicero and Caesar, Pliny and Tacitus, Diodorus Siculus and Strabo, speak in high terms. In the Druidic order indeed centred, and from it radiated, the whole civil and ecclesiastical knowledge of the realm: they were its statesmen, legislators, priests, physicians, lawyers, teachers, poets; the depositaries of all human and divine knowledge; its Church and parliaments; its courts of law; its colleges of physicians and surgeons; its magistrates, clergy and bishops. The number of Druids was regulated by very stringent laws in proportion to the population. None could be a candidate for the Order who could not, in the May congress of the tribe, prove his descent from nine successive generations of free forefathers. No slave could of course be a Druid; becoming one, he forfeited his Order and privileges; and hence perhaps one of the reasons of the protracted, stubborn, and finally successful resistance of the Druidic island to the Roman arms; for it was not till the reign of Adrian, A.D. 120, that Britain was incorporated, and then by treaty, not conquest, with the Roman dominions, the Britons retaining their kings, land, laws and rights, and stipulating in return to raise and support three legions to be officered by the Emperor for the defence of the common empire. [16] By common law every Briton was seized as his birthright of five acres (ten English) of land in the gweli cenedl, the 'bed' or hereditary county of his clan. If the clan land was exhausted, recourse was had to emigration or conquest, and for this purpose the superfluous population was draughted off as an army, or more generally as a colony. Hence the mother-tribe and daughter-tribes of the same name which so frequently occur in Britain, Gaul, Germany and Hibernia. In addition to these five acres, the Druid received five acres more and a certain fixed income from his tribe. The difficulty of admission into the Order was on a par with its privileges. The head of the clan possessed a veto on every ordination. Every candidate was obliged to find twelve head of families as sureties for moral conduct and adequate maintenance; nor could he be ordained until he had passed three examinations three successive years before the Druidic college of the tribe. These barriers to promiscuous admission threw the Order almost entirely into the hands of the blaenorion, or aristocracy, making it literally a "royal priesthood," kings, princes, and nobles entering largely into its composition. "All power," states Caesar, speaking of Gaul, "is vested in the two orders of the Druids and aristocracy: the people are nothing." This, however, was evidently not the case in Britain, where the primitive Druidic laws, unaffected hitherto by foreign innovations, referred the source of all power to the people in congress, and every congress was opened with the words *Trech gwlad n' arglwydd,* 'The country is above the king.' Nevertheless, the authority and influence of the Druids were very great, and, on the whole, as popular as they were great. The extreme penalty lodged in their hands, and the one most dreaded, was that of excommunication — *poena gravissima,* states Caesar — which was, in fact, a decree of expulsion from both worlds, the present and future. The terror it inspired is the best proof that it was not abused and but rarely resorted to; for the most terrific punishments, if abused, soon lose their effect and become despised.

The sacred animal of Druidism was the white astral bull; the sacred bird, the crested wren; the sacred tree, the oak; the sacred grain, wheat; the sacred plant, the mistletoe; the sacred herbs, the trefoil, vervain, and hyssop.

The great festivals of Druidism were three: the vernal, on the 1st of May; the autumnal; and the midwinter, when the mistletoe was gathered by the arch-Druids. The mistletoe, with its three white berries, was the symbol of the Druidic Trinity, and its growth in the oak the type of the incarnation of the Deity in man.

The hypaethral altar in the Druidic circle was called cromlech (stone of bowing, or adoration). Near it another stone received in a cavity water direct from heaven (holy water.) This holy water and the waters of the river Dee, the Jordan of ancient Britain, were the only waters permitted to be used in Druidic sacrifices. No Druid could wear arms of any description. None but a Druid could officiate at a sacrifice.

The canonicals of the Druid were white linen robes, no metal but gold being used in any part of the dress. The canonicals of the arch-Druids were extremely gorgeous, not very dissimilar from those of the high-priest of the Hebrew religion. The Druidic cross was wrought in gold down the length of the back of his robe.

No Druidic service could be celebrated before sunrise or after sunset.

The Druidic was essentially a priesthood of peace, neither wearing arms nor permitting arms to be unsheathed in its presence; and though patriotism, or the defence of one's country in a just war, was a high virtue in its system, we have no instance of Druidism persecuting or using physical force against any other religion or set of opinions. Its whole theory, indeed, would have stultified itself in so doing; and herein consists no small part of its identity with Christianity. [17]

The saying of Taliesin, the prince-Bard and Druid, conveys a great historic truth, though over-strongly expressed: — "Christ, the Word from the beginning, was from the beginning our teacher, and we never lost His teaching. Christianity was a new thing in Asia, but there never was a time when the Druids of Britain held not its doctrines."

Having thus passed in review the religious status of our own country, in the apostolic era, we proceed to give an epitome of the events in British history which brought the royal family of Britain into contact with St. Paul at Rome.

[1] Artemidorus, quoted by Strabo, the Orphic Hymns; Avienus de Britannia.
[2] There is touching beauty in many of the Druidic triads, as in the following: — "There are three men all should love: He that loves the face of his mother Nature; he that loves rational works of art; he that looks lovingly on the faces of little children."
[3] The symbol of Druidism in Crete was the Menw-tarw, or Menw-bull and its chief temple the Labyrinth. Out of such simple elements the imaginative Greek mind forged the fable of Minos, the Minotaur, and the Pasiphae, as it did that of the rape of Europa from the Astarte of Syria.
[4] Sir John Fortescue, *De Laudibus Legum Angliae;* Coke, Preface to third vol. of Pleadings; Origin of the Common Law of England.
[5] There are now three states of existence; the cycle of 'Ceugant,' where there is nothing of living or dead but God, and God alone can traverse it; the cycle of 'Abred,' where all natural existence originates from death — this man has traversed; the cycle of 'Gwynfyd,' where all existence is from life to life — this man will traverse in the 'Nevoedd' (changes of life in heaven)...The Druids, contrary to the Mosaic account, made the creation of man simultaneous with that of solar light. "Three things came into being at the same moment — light, man, and moral choice." — (Druidic Triads.)

[6] So Procopius also testifies: —

"Hesus, Taranis Belenus unus tantummodo Deus
Unum Deum Dominum universi Druides Solum agnoscimt."

De Gothicis, lib. iii.

[7] The Druid regarded himself as the priest of the deity of nature, but in addition to this hierarchic character there appears to have been the following observances derived from one original family, language, and religion common to his with all the other forms of the primitive truth — libation, sacrifices, tradition of the Deluge, of the war of the Titanidae against Heaven, metempsychosis, adoration towards the East, the division of the circle into 360 degrees, of the zodiac into twelve signs, of the week into seven days. Most of these we find in the Chaldaean faith, and it is certain the Chaldaeans were highly civilised 2,000 years before the Christian era.

[8] The three causes of man falling into 'Abred' — neglect of knowledge, aversion to good, love of evil. Occasioned by these three, man declines to his congenial state in 'abred,' whence as before he re-ascends to humanity. (Druidic Triads.)

[9] The three things God alone can do — endure the eternities of infinity, participate of all being without changing, renew everything without annihilating it. The three things wherein man necessarily differs from God — man is finite, God infinite; man had a beginning, God had none; man unable to sustain 'ceugant' (infinity of space and time), must have in 'gwynfyd' eternal change, cycles of existence; God sustains 'ceupan' unchanged. (Druidic Triads.)

[10] Three things decrease continually, darkness, evil, and death. Three things increase continually, light, truth, and life. These will finally prevail over all; then 'abred' will end. (Druidic Triads.) The idea of the eternal progression of man and the universe which pervades the Triads is very fine.

[11] A Druidic Catechism, of which fragments only are extant.

[12] The three necessary essentials of God — infinite in Himself, finite to the finite, co-unity with every model of existence in 'gwynfyd.' (Druidic Triads.)

[13] There could in fact, according to the Druids, be no life at all in 'abred' except as proceeding from death. Above 'abred' death ceased, and the celestial novations ran through eternity.

[14] The Gildas MS. (Julius, D. xi.), Cottonian Library, calls these the three archflamens and twenty-eight flamens of Britain. Geoffrey of Monmouth appears to have found the same titles in the Armorican version of Tyssiiio's History.

[15] "He that will be a prophet of God," writes Gildas, "must never rest till he has traced everything to its cause and mode of operation. He will then know what God does, for God does nothing but what should be, in the manner it should be, at the time and in the order it should be. By understanding these laws of God, he will be able to see and foretell the future." (*Principles of Prediction of Gildas the Prophet, Iolo* MSS., p. 609.) Prophecy, then, was with the Druids nothing but the theological term for science, and Gildas supplies a useful commentary on Caesar's words: "The Druids discuss many things concerning the stars and their revolutions, the magnitude of the globe and its various divisions, the nature of the universe, the energy and power of the immortal gods." (*Caesar's Com.*, lib. v.)

[16] The accepting or circulating of Roman coin in Britain was made a capital offence by Arviragus; for such an act according to the Roman construction, inferred the right of levying tribute, as we see in the Scriptures: "Whose image and superscription is this? Caesar's. Render therefore unto Caesar the things that are Caesar's." From the reign of Claudius to that of Hadrian no coins, therefore, of the intervening Roman emperors have been found in Britain. From Hadrian onward there have been found a nearly complete series.

[17] "In the ancient world," observes Higgins (Celtic Researches, p. 196), "the Druids were the only priesthood of peace. Clad in his white canonicals, the Druidic herald presented himself between two armies, and every sword was instantly sheathed."

Chapter Two - Historic Positions of Britain and the Roman Empire at the Commencement of the Christian Era

Julius Caesar, in justification of his invasion of Britain, alleges the Britons to have been the aggressors, British levies taking the field against him in every Gallic campaign. Those singular collections of cardinal events known as the "Triads of the Isle of Britain," corroborate the statement. Prior to Caesar's campaigns in Northern Gaul, a British army of 50,000 men, termed in these Triads the "second silver host," under the command of the two nephews of Cassibelaunus, or Caswàllon, invaded Aquitania, routed the Roman proconsul, Lucius Valerius Praeconinus, at Tolosa, and compelled Lucius Manilius, the consul, to fly with the loss of all his commissariat. On receiving intelligence of these reverses, Caesar turned his arms against the Veneti (Vendeans), who carried on a flourishing commerce with Britain, and whose navy supplied the transport for these auxiliaries. As long as the Venetine fleet, which from Caesar's description of it would do no discredit to our present state of nautical architecture, remained mistress of the narrow seas, invasion was impracticable. Upon its destruction, Caesar advanced by slow marches to Portius Iccius (Witsand), near Calais, and on the 5th of August, B.C. 55, the Roman fleet crossed the Channel in two divisions. This first campaign lasted fifty-five days, during which Caesar failed to advance beyond seven miles from the spot of disembarkation, lost one battle, and had his camp attempted by the victorious enemy, a thing unprecedented in his continental career. [1]

The second expedition embarked in above a thousand ships, and carrying the army which afterwards completed the conquest of the world on the fields of Pharsalia and Munda, set sail from Witsand May 10, B.C. 54. The campaign lasted till September 10, when peace was concluded at

Gwerddlan (Verulam, or St. Albans), the furthest point (70 miles) from the coast Caesar had been able to attain. The conditions are not particularized in either the Triads or Commentaries. Hostages and a tribute are mentioned by Caesar, but it is certain from numerous passages in the Augustan authors that no Briton of eminence left the island a hostage or prisoner. On the conclusion of the treaty, Caesar moved from Verulam to London, where he was entertained at the Bryn Gwyn (white mount) [2] by Cassibelaunus, the British pendràgon, or military dictator, with a magnificence which appears to have found great favour in the eyes of the ancient Bards, who record it with great exactness. Leaving not a Roman soldier behind, Caesar disembarked his forces at Rutupium, at ten at night, and arrived at Witsand by daybreak the next morning, September 20, B.C. 54.

The tests of the success or non-success of a campaign are its effects. The effects of the second Julian invasion demonstrate that both at Rome and in Gaul it was considered a more serious failure than the first. The line quoted by Lucan —

"*Territa quaesitis ostendit terga Britannus*" [3]
as a common sarcasm in the mouths of the Pompeian party against Caesar, may be thrown aside as the invidious exaggeration of the defeat on the Darent, and the loss of his sword to Nennius, the brother of Caswàllon; but it is undeniable that the invasion cost Caesar for a time the loss of all his continental acquisitions. Before he could dispose of his troops in winter quarters, the Treviro, Eburones, Senones, and Sicambri rose in arms, and the work of Gallic conquest had to be re-enacted.

To estimate aright the military abilities of Caswàllon, and the resources of the British people at this period of the first collision of our island with the continent, it should be borne in mind that they were engaged against perhaps the ablest general of antiquity, heading an army to which, either before or after the invasion, France, Spain, Western Germany, Africa, Egypt, Asia, and finally Rome itself succumbed; the conquerors, in fact, of Europe, Asia, and Africa, and the real founders of the imperial dynasty of the Caesars. The double repulsion of the Julian expedition by the ancient Britons has never received due weight or consideration. It yet remains unparalleled in British history.

Barbarism is a very indefinite term. To the Greeks and Romans all other nations were in common parlance "barbarians," by which was meant no more than "foreigners." If popular amusements are to be taken as the test, the Romans were themselves the most barbarous of the nations of Europe. The Coliseum is the gigantic evidence of the race of human wolves which they not unaptly considered themselves to be. When the brutal sports of the gladiators were proposed to be introduced at Athens, even the Cynic philosopher cried out, "We must first pull down the statue to

Mercy which our forefathers erected fifteen hundred years ago." A similar gulf separated the British from the Roman temper, and the accounts of the latter people with regard to the former must be received with much the same caution as those of the modern enemies of the same reserved and incommunicative insular race. Boadicea, in her oration as given by Dion Cassius, observes, that though Britain had been for a century open to the continent, yet its language, philosophy, and usages continued as great a mystery as ever to the Romans themselves; and the same remark, with little modification, applies still. All the evidences supplied by Caesar refute the notion of material barbarism. Agriculture was universal, corn everywhere abundant, pasturage a distinct branch of national wealth, the population so thick as to excite his astonishment — "infinita multitudo hominum" — the surest and most satisfactory proof of a sound social state and ample means of sustenance. [4] The points which appear to have originated the idea of barbarism connected in some minds with the ancient Britons are, that they stripped to fight, which every Briton, every British schoolboy continues to do, and no other nation does; and, secondly, that they tattooed their bodies with various devices in deep blue lines, a practice which the British sailor cherishes in all its original freedom, and from which probably he will never be weaned, for these immemorial usages seemed rooted in something much deeper than taste or imitation. Our soldiers also still retain the propensity of getting rid of every accoutrement and incumbrance in battle, and of charging as naked as military regulations will allow them. Yet it would be ridiculous to term our sailors and soldiers barbarians in the modern sense of the word because they continue in these respects to be "true blue ancient Briton." In all the solid essentials of humanity our British ancestors will compare to great advantage with the best eras of Greece or Rome. In war the Briton, after the Julian invasions, walked the streets of Rome the only freeman in Europe, pointed at as the exception to the world: —

"Invictus Romano Marte Britannus." [5]

For ninety-seven years no Roman again ventured to set hostile foot on the island, and when the eagle of Romulus once more expanded its pinions to the stormy winds of ocean, it was when no other enemy, unconquered, confronted its gaze from the Euphrates to Gibraltar, and the forces of the whole empire were ready to follow its leading against the solitary free nationality of the West.

Caswàllon, the able antagonist of Caesar, reigned after the invasion seven years. Augustus Caesar succeeded Julius B.C. 30. Henceforth Rome is to be regarded as the unity of the continent of Europe, Northern Africa, and Asia, in action from a central court under a series of autocrats rarely swerving from the imperial policy laid down by the Julian family. Augustus sent ambassadors to Britain demanding the restoration of the three Reguli of the Coritani, or Coraniaid, Dumno, Belaunus, and Jernian, to their estates, confiscated for treason. Tenuantius, the son of Caswàllon, a mild, pacific monarch, had sent his two sons, Cynvèlin and Llyr (Lear), to be educated at Rome, where they were brought up with his nephews in his palace by Augustus himself, who made a rule, as Suetonius informs us, of teaching the younger branches of his family in person. Cynvèlin subsequently served in the German campaigns under Germanicus. He had now succeeded his father, and received the Roman ambassadors with courtesy, but peremptorily rejected the interference of a foreign potentate in the affairs of the island. Augustus moved half the disposable forces of the empire to the Gallic harbours on the Channel, but he never entertained serious intentions of an invasion. Cynvèlin concentrated his army at Dover. A British fleet, as we learn from Dion Cassius, swept the Channel. The preparations of Augustus, tardily urged, indicated that prudential motives had already superseded the suggestions of pride. He had never conducted his campaigns in person, and where the genius of Julius had been baffled, inferior skill was likely to incur nought but disgrace and disaster. A reverse, as Horace had the courage to warn him (Ode 35, lib. v.), would be followed by a rising of the oligarchic faction in Italy. Cynvèlin was not slow to take advantage of this reluctancy. A conference with the imperial friend and tutor of his youth was solicited. The result was the triumph of British diplomacy, a much rarer success than that of the British arms. Not only did the emperor abandon his demands, but the heavy duties previously levied on British goods were reduced to a very light tariff (Strabo, lib. iv. c. 5). Friendly relations were restored. British nobles again took up their residence at Rome, and were to be seen dedicating their offerings at the shrines of the Capitol.

Cymbeline, or Cynvèlin, after a reign of thirty-five years, was succeeded by his eldest son Cuiderius (Gwyddyr), his younger, Arviragus (Gweyrydd), receiving the dukedom of Cornwall (Cernyw), which by the British laws was a dukedom royal. The numerous coins of Cynvèlin (Cunobelinus) which remain in our days, are the only monuments we possess of a national mint in Western Europe apart from that of Rome. The horse, sometimes thought to be introduced as a national emblem by the Saxons, is one of the most common types upon them, Britain being long before the reign of Cymbeline famous for its breed of steeds, and the daring and accomplishments of its charioteers.

We now enter the times contemporary with St. Paul.

As the central figure in the group of the historic characters we are about to portray is Caràdoc, king of Siluria, we are called upon to notice somewhat at large his birth and character. [6]

It is a matter of wonder and indignation how few patriotic heroes the long annals of history present to our view. One in a century is not to be found. Turning over the pages which record the aggressions of the Romans on various nations, we inquire in vain for the most part for heroes to confront them. When we have named a Viriathus for Spain, a Hannibal for Carthage, an Arminius or Herman for Germany, a Mithridates for Asia, we have exhausted the catalogue of three continents. Britain is here also an exception to the world, for it shews an almost uninterrupted succession of patriots of the highest order, from Caswàllon and Caràdoc, through the Arthurs and Cadwallos, to the Wallaces and Glyndores of the Norman period. Nor have we any wars on record so long and stubborn as those which were waged, first between the Britons and the Romans, and secondly between the same Britons and the Saxons with other Teuton tribes, after the fall of the great empire. But Caràdoc stands forth preeminently as the ideal of what a patriot in the field should be. With Arminius the last spark of liberty had expired on the Continent. Northern Africa had finally been incorporated, by the arms of Suetonius, Paulinus, and Cneius Geta, into the Roman Empire. Gaul, Spain, Southern Germany, Italy, Eastern Europe, and Asia as far as the Euphrates enjoyed profound peace and no small amount of material prosperity under the enormous shadow of the Roman Capitol. The Caesars were seated, firm as the seven hills themselves, on the throne. East and west, north and south, there was no enemy to be encountered; all was subjection and repose. The formidable armies of the imperial state hung up their shields for lack of a foe, or were employed in the formation of the numerous military roads which radiated like a network from Rome to Finisterre and Calais westward, and to the shores of the Persian Gulf eastward. It was in truth the grandest and most magnificent of empires, the extent of which, though embracing 1,600,000 sq. miles, and a population of 120,000,000 of Caucasian or semi-Caucasian blood, was its least glory. Nothing has risen like it since. Its mere fragments have sufficed for modern kingdoms. Countries ruled by proconsuls now term their rulers emperors. Fertile and well-cultivated, not only were these countries situated in the healthiest part of the temperate zone, but they teemed with all the materials of the finest soldiery, with all the resources of inexhaustible physical wealth. "Urbs Roma orbs humana" was no unfounded boast, for within the circumference of the empire were contained almost every land and race that had contributed to the civilization and progress of humanity. All the appliances of this vast unity of law and arms were at the command of one despot, and were now about to be moved towards the northern harbours of Gaul for the invasion of the only unconquered land of the ancient civilization.

One army and one general constituted the force which Caswàllon was called upon to resist; but Caràdoc was summoned by the voice of his country to take the field against an empire pouring forth a succession of armies in the highest state of discipline, under a succession of able and experienced commanders. This is the first time Britain was matched against the world in arms, and right nobly did the little island acquit herself.

Brân, or Brennus, the father of Caràdoc, was the son of Llyr, brother of Cynvèlin, surnamed Llyr Llediaith, from the foreign accent imparted to the pronunciation of his native tongue by his education under Augustus at Rome. During threatened invasion of Augustus he commanded the British fleet in the Channel. Augustus was succeeded by Tiberius Claudius Caesar, and Tiberius by Caligula, A.D. 37, a year marked by the births of Nero, Josephus the Jewish historian, and Julius Agricola, the future commander of the Roman forces in Britain. The tranquility pervading the empire instigated Caligula to renew the attempts at a conquest which the first and second Caesars had either failed to achieve, or prudently bequeathed to their successors. The character, however, of this emperor, compounded of mania and vice, left a memorable stamp of ridicule upon the whole expedition. The armies of Gaul and the Rhine rendezvoused at Boulogne. A Roman flotilla collected from the Spanish ports was moored, ostensibly prepared to embark the troops, in the Seine. The appearance, however, of a British fleet under Arviragus disconcerted and put an abrupt end to the enterprize, if indeed it was ever seriously meditated. Caligula, who felt a morbid gratification in burlesqueing the most momentous measures of state, and scandalizing his subjects by the maddest freaks of imperial caprice, held a grand review of his splendid expeditionary force on the sands at Boulogne. At its termination, ascending the tribunal, he expiated on the glory which already encircled his brow as one who had led his troops like Bacchus, Hercules, and Sesostris, to the confines of the earth-surrounding ocean. He asked if such renown ought to be jeopardized by an armed exploration of an island which nature itself had removed beyond the power and jurisdiction of the gods of Rome, and which the campaigns of the deified Caesar himself had only succeeded in pointing out to the wonder of the continental world. "Let us, my comrades," he continued, adopting the well known phrase of the great Julius (*commilitones*), "leave these Britons unmolested. To war beyond the bounds of nature is not courage, but impiety. Let us rather load ourselves with the bloodless spoils of the Atlantic ocean which the same beneficent goddess of nature pours on these sands so lavishly at our feet. Follow the example of your emperor — behold," he added, suiting the action to the word, "I wreathe for laurel this garland of green sea-weed around my immortal brow, and for *spolia optima* I fill my helm with these smooth and brilliant shells. Decorated with these we will return to Rome, and, instead of a British king, Neptune and Nereus, the gods of ocean themselves, shall follow captives to the Capitol behind our triumphal car. To each of you, my fellow soldiers in this arduous enterprize, I promise a gratuity of a year's extra stipend in merited acknowledgment of your services and fidelity to your emperor."

This singular harangue, which we are tempted to regard as the practical sarcasm of a despot not altogether insane on the ambition of the whole race of conquerors, was welcomed with thunders of acclamation. The projected expedition had been from the first viewed with extreme distaste by the soldiery, and despite the indignation openly expressed by the officers, they did not hesitate to give vent to their satisfaction, and, with military jests and peals of laughter, imitate the example of their imperial master. The British fleet gazed with astonishment on these bronzed and mail-clad veterans disporting themselves in the childish amusement of collecting shells on the seashore. The camp was broken up, and Caligula entered Rome in triumphal procession, with his army, on his birthday, August 31, A.D. 40. He was assassinated next year, in the 29th year of his age (January 24th), and succeeded by Claudius, then in his 50th year.

The father of Tiberius Claudius Caesar was Drusus Claudius Nero, elevated first to the quaestorship, then to the praetorship, subsequently appointed to conduct the Rhaetian and German campaigns. He was the first Roman commander that navigated in force the German Ocean. He carried his arms to the centre of Germany, and is stated by Suetonius to have been deterred from further advance by the sudden apparition on his march of a female of more than mortal stature and beauty, bidding him halt the Roman banners where she appeared. He died suddenly, not without suspicion of foul play, in the Castra ^Estiva, thence called Scelerata, whilst preparing to extend his conquests in another direction. His body was conveyed from town to town, and buried with state honours, Augustus himself pronouncing the funeral panegyric, in the Campus Martius at Rome. Nearly connected as he was with the Caesars, Drusus remained to the last a stern republican. He left three children, Germanicus, Livilla, and Claudius; the last born at Lyons. The infancy, childhood, and youth of the future emperor were spent under the strictest state of surveillance. He was regarded as but one remove from an idiot. "He is as imbecile as my son Claudius" was an ordinary phrase in his mother Livia's mouth when she wished to imply an extraordinary degree of stupidity. His appearance did not belie his character. Tall and full in person, and possessed, when seated, of the external show of dignity, in motion his knees shook, his head perpetually trembled, his tongue stuttered, his laughter was outrageously violent, and his anger marked by profuse foaming at the mouth. Cruel and bloodthirsty by nature, as indeed every Roman was, he insisted on being present whenever any criminal was put to the torture. He never failed to give the sign of "no quarter" against disabled gladiators, and delighted with a horrible voracity to gloat over the dying expression of their faces. He sat from morning to night, neglecting the ordinary hours of refreshment, at the *bestiaria,* or combats of wild beasts, and yet personally was the rankest and most contemptible of cowards. He never attended an invitation except surrounded by guards, who searched every guest before he entered the apartment, a precaution exercised on every citizen who accosted him. In many points there exists a strong resemblance between Claudius and our James the First — both were addicted to the lowest companions and buffoonery, both were poltroons, both coarse gourmands, and both were pedants of the deepest dye. Yet it must be confessed that the loss of the work of Claudius on the Races and Antiquities of Primitive Italy is one that can never be replaced, the few fragments we possess evincing it to have been a mine of undigested, but very valuable and authentic matter.

Let us with the Roman emperor contrast the British patriot. Caractacus was born at Trevran, the seat of his father Bran, within the present parish of Llanilid, in Glamorganshire. He received his education at the Druidic cor of Caerleon-on-Usk, where most of the Silurian nobility were trained in the cycle of Celtic accomplishments. Of these, oratory was one of the chief, and we possess in the speech of the British king before Claudius a fair specimen of the bold, free, terse style inculcated in these ancient national colleges. Allusion is made in it to a long line of illustrious ancestors — "clari majores." It sounds strange to persons accustomed to think a Norman pedigree, dating from A.D. 1066, ancient, to hear this British king, a thousand years before, face to face with a Roman emperor, and in the heart of the Capitol deliver himself proudly of a royal lineage, the fount of which, like that of the Nile, was lost in its very remoteness. In the clan times, however, the preservation of a pedigree meant the preservation of all that was valuable in blood, station, and property. Without it a man was an outlaw; he had no clan, consequently no legal rights or status. Genealogies were guarded, therefore, with extreme jealousy, and recorded with painful exactitude by the herald-bards of each clan. On the public reception, at the age of fifteen, of a child into the clan, his family genealogy was proclaimed, and all challengers of it commanded to come forward. Pedigree and inheritance, indeed, were so identified in the ancient British code, that an heir even in the ninth descent could redeem at a jury valuation any portion of an hereditary estate from which necessity had compelled his forefathers to part. As the succession of these *clari majores* may be interesting to the antiquary, we extract it from the Pantliwydd Manuscripts of Llansannor: —

"*Genealogy of Carádoc.* Carádoc ab Brân Fendigaid, ab Llyr Llediaith, ab Baran, ab Ceri Hirlyn Gwyn, ab Caid, ab Arch, ab Meirion, ab Ceraint, ab

Greidiol, ab Dingad, ab Anyn, ab Alafon, ab Brywlais, ab Ceraint Feddw, ab Berwyn, ab Morgan, ab Bleddyn, ab Rhun, ab Idwal, ab Llywarch, ab Calchwynydd, ab Enir Fardd, ab Ithel, ab Llarian, ab Teuged, ab Llyfeinydd, ab Peredur, ab Gweyrydd, ab Ithon, ab Cymryw, ab Brwt, ab Selys Hên, ab Annyn Tro, ab Brydain, ab Aedd Mawr."

Reckoning thirty years for a generation, this pedigree carries us back 1,080 years, that is, 330 years before the foundation of Rome. Not all of these ancestors have escaped the reprobation of the blunt Bardic chroniclers — one of them especially, Ceraint Feddw, is stigmatized as an irreclaimable drunkard, deposed by his subjects for setting fire just before harvest to the corn lands of Siluria. In the year A.D. 36, Brân resigned the Silurian crown to Caràdoc, and became Arch-Druid of the college of Siluria, where he remained till called upon to be a hostage for his son. At the period of his accession Caràdoc had three sons, Cyllin or Cyllinus, Lleyn or Linus, and Cynon, and two daughters, Eurgain and Gladys, or Claudia.

In July, A.D. 42, a British embassy arrived at Rome from Guiderius, complaining of the encouragement extended by the Emperor to the intrigues of Beric and Adminius, two *reguli* of the Brigantes and Coritani, who, in consequence of being detected in a treasonable correspondence with Caligula during the late menaced invasion, had been banished by Britain. Claudius had powerful reasons for declining to receive the ambassadors. The invasion of Britain had been already decided upon, and the Roman forces were collecting at the usual rendezvous at Boulogne.

Whatever the deficiencies of the Emperor himself might be, at no time were the great offices of state filled by men of higher administrative capacity, or better able to wield the vast military resources of the empire. Aulus Plautius, a general who emulated the Scipios in the rigour of his discipline and the rapidity of his marches, was appointed to the command of the army of invasion. The fleet and transports collected were too numerous and well appointed for the British naval force to cope with, and it accordingly returned to Torbay. This obstacle was no sooner removed, than another, quite unparalleled in the annals of Roman obedience, arose. The army refused to embark, and broke into open mutiny. Appeals to their sacraments, or military oaths of allegiance, failed to move them, the only response they elicited being, "We will march anywhere *in* the world, but not *out* of it." The lapse of ninety years had not extinguished the memory of the Julian campaigns, the sanguinary disembarkation on the Walmer beach, the stubborn battle-fields, and the terrible chariotcharges. Intelligence of this alarming state of things soon reached Rome, and Claudius at once despatched his favourite freedman and minister, Narcissus, to the scene of disaffection. Convening the army, Narcissus, whose failings were not those of moral or physical cowardice, mounted the general's tribune and commenced his harangue. It was the first time a eunuch had ever dared to address Roman soldiers. Stupefaction and indignation for a time kept the legions dumb, but when he exclaimed "He would himself lead them into Britain," a universal shout of execration arose, and rushing to the tent of Plautius, they called upon him to give the signal for embarkation. Taking instant advantage of this change of temper, Plautius embarked the army in three divisions, and landed two days afterwards at Rutupium, or Ynys Ruthin, between Thanet and Richborough.

From Dover to Holyhead ran the British causeway, constructed by Dyfnwal and his son, Beli the Great, B.C. 400, called Sarn Wyddèlin, or the Irish Road, Wyddèlin being the British term for 'Irish.' The corruption into Watling Street is not great. Along the Sarn Wyddelin Caesar had directed his march, and Plautius moved his forces on the same line. He found the British army drawn up under Guiderius and Caràdoc at Southfleet, across the Sarn on the flat between the Kentish hills and the Thames. The action terminated in the Britons falling back to Wimbledon Heath, where a second battle was fought, in which Guiderius fell. He was succeeded on the throne by his brother Arviragus, but the national emergency requiring the establishment of the pendragonate, or military dictatorship, Caràdoc was unanimously elected to that high office, Arviragus giving his vote first in his favour, and consenting to act under him. Caràdoc withdrew his forces across the Thames at Chertsey, Plautius following along the Sarn, now called "The Devil's Causeway." In attempting to force the passage of the Thames at Kingston, the Roman general was thrice foiled. He then proceeded to Silchester, by means of his German cavalry defeated a British division at Nettlebed, in Oxfordshire, and returning by a forced march to Wallingford, crossed the Thames there, after a desperate resistance. Dion Cassius, the Greek historian, gives a vivid description of the action. The Romans, led by Plautius, Flavius Vespasian, the future emperor, and his brother, entered the river in three columns, whilst the German cavalry swam it lower down, and assailed the British position in flank. But the British stupidity, which never knows when it is beaten, appears to be of very old date. Dion states the contest continued with slight intermissions for two whole days on the northern side, and that the defeat of Caràdoc was eventually effected by a daring mancevre on his flank and rear made by Cneius Geta, the conqueror of Mauritania, who was rewarded for it, though he had not yet attained the consular dignity, with the honours of a triumph. It tells well for the abilities of Caràdoc that in this first battle as pendragon he was able to hold his ground for two days of incessant fighting against three such generals as Plautius, Vespasian, and Geta. Undismayed, he collected his forces again, and Plautius, on attempting to follow him, was so roughly handled that messages were sent to Rome for instructions and reinforcements. Claudius himself immediately quitted Rome, and passing through Gaul, landed at Richborough, with the second and fourteenth legions, their auxiliaries, and a cohors of elephants brought over for the express purpose of neutralizing the British chariot-charges. He effected a junction with Plautius at Verulam. Beric and Adminius had accompanied him, and, as had been previously arranged, the two states of the Iceni and Coritani, or Coraniaid, on their making their appearance among them, rose in arms and proclaimed their alliance with the invaders, Caràdoc had thus the Romans in front and an insurgent country in the rear. Dion terms Caer Col, or Colchester, the *basileion* or royal residence of Cynvèlin. It was known at this period as Comulodunum, the city of Camul, an Umbric or Cymric term for the God of War. [7] In its defence Caràdoc fought two more battles— the first at Coxall Knolls, and the second at Brandon camp, on the Teme. In this latter the horses of the British chariots, the odour of elephants being insupportable to this animal, gave way in all directions, and Caràdoc suffered his first decisive defeat. Colchester in a few days surrendered. A treaty was concluded, known as the Claudian treaty, by which it was stipulated that the Coranidae and Iceni, on the payment of a certain amount of tribute, should, under the Roman protectorate, be guaranteed their land, laws, and native government. Claudius is said to have promised also his natural daughter, Venus Julia, called in the British accounts Venissa, to Arviragus. The alliance in after years took place, and Arviragus built Caer Gloyw, or Gloucester, in honour of his imperial father-in-law. Claudius left the further prosecution of the war to his generals, and, returning to Rome, celebrated his triumph with signal magnificence — the more impressive from the humility displayed by himself in ascending the steps of the Capitol on his knees, supported on either side by his sons-in-law. But the war had in reality only just begun. Caràdoc, having carried fire and sword through the territories of the revolted tribes, transferred hostilities from the champaigns of the eastern counties to the hilly districts of the southwest. Here he proceeded to levy and arm fresh forces. It is instructive to study the movements on both sides, for never was war carried on with greater energy and laboriousness. Plautius marched against the pendràgon by land, whilst Vespasian was dispatched with the Roman fleet to effect a landing at Torbay. Geta was left at Colchester, his legions commencing the construction of that celebrated line of fortresses which extended from the head of the fens, now forming the Isle of Ely, to Gloucester. This immense work, the object of which was to mark off southern Britain at once as a Roman province, was carried on day and night with the usual indefatigability and science of the Roman service. Castra after castra rose, each as completed being occupied by its appropriate garrison, and the British pendràgon heard at the same time of the rising of the formidable circumvallation in his rear, of the advance of Plautius on his flank, and the disembarkation of Vespasion in his front. Devonshire (*Dyvnaint,* the deep vales), Dorset (the water land), and Somerset (*Gwlad yr hav, summerland*), were, however, admirably adapted for the display of British intrepidity and tactics. The camps, Roman and British, pitched at almost regular intervals in hostile frontage of each other over the whole surface of these counties, bespeak better than any history the desperate and long-sustained character of the campaigns which now ensued. In the art of castrametation we fail to detect any evidence of scientific superiority on the part of the invaders, it appears to us to be, if anywhere, on the British side, especially in the ramparts and in the strength of the approaches. But it is certain that both the British and Roman soldier must have been in the highest condition of military discipline before earthworks necessitating such labour to construct and such vigilence to defend could have been carried out as part of the ordinary drill of the day. The 'navvy' power displayed in them is not unworthy of the present century. Here the war rolled backward and forward for seven years, absorbing during that time the almost undivided military interest of the Roman world; for, with the exception of the rebellion, soon crushed out by Corbulo, in Armenia, the British pendragon was bearing the whole brunt of the arms of the empire, under a series of its finest generals. In these seven years, according to Suetonius thirty, according to Eutropius thirty-two battles were fought. The central camp of Plautius was fixed between Silbury Hill and Amesbury, that of Vespasian and his son Titus on Hampden Hill, near Ilchester, the area of which was able to accommodate 100,000 men. On the ground now forming a farm called Conquest-farm, Bishops Lydiard, near a smaller camp of twenty acres, Arviragus sustained a total defeat by Vespasian, who proceeded to invest Caer Use (Exeter). On the eighth day of the siege he was surprised in his intrenchments by Caràdoc and Arviragus, and routed with great slaughter. Titus had on this occasion the glory of saving his father's life. The British attack was so sudden that Vespasian was on the point of being slain in his tent, when Titus, divining his father's danger, charged his captors at the head of the first cohort of the fourteenth legion, and rescued him from their hands. [8]

Plautius, Vespasian, Geta, and Titus were successively recalled. We cannot do better than use the significant language of Tacitus in describing the fluctuations of the war, victory hovering now over the Romans, now over the British standards: — "The Silures reposed unbounded confidence in Caractacus, enumerating the many drawn battles he had fought with the Romans, the many victories he had obtained over them." 9 The passionate attachment, indeed, of his countrymen to their high-souled and incorruptible compatriot is abundantly evidenced by the fond allusions to him in their ancient Triads. "Three have been," declare these records, "our hero-kings — Cynvèlin, Caràdoc, Arthur. Except by treachery they could not be overthrown." "Three have been the chief battle-kings of the Isle of Britain — Caswàllon, son of Beli; Arviragus, son of Cynvèlin; Caràdoc, son of Brân." "Caràdoc, son of Brân, whom every Briton, from the king to the peasant, followed when he lifted his spear to battle."

But we must draw his military career, which is but indirectly connected with this essay, to a close. On the recall of Plautius, who had married Gladys (Pomponia Graecina), the sister of Caractacus, a truce was concluded for six months, during which must be fixed the visit of the British chief to Rome. What credence to attach to the British story in the Iolo MSS., which represents him as appearing before the senate, and stating that he had ordered "every tree in Siluria to be felled, that the Romans might no longer allege it was the British forests, and not British valour, which baffled him," we hardly know. It is in accordance with his character, which we recognise also in the anecdote recorded by Dion. "When Caractacus," says that historian, "was shewn the public buildings of Rome, he observed, 'It is singular a people possessed of such magnificence at home should envy me my soldier's tent in Britain.' "On the expiration of the truce and the return of Caràdoc to his command, Ostorius Scapula, with the Plautian line of fortresses for his base of operations, proceeded to carry the war westward. Supported by the Silures and Ordovicians, the fierce indomitable mountaineers, whom the Roman arms never succeeded in subduing, the Pendragon contested every advance of the invaders. Around Caer Essylt (the Hereford Beacon) a succession of encounters took place for six months. The winter did not interrupt hostilities. A Roman division which had penetrated as far as Caerleon was cut to pieces. Ostorius, in the next campaign, fixed his headquarters at Castra Ostorii, in Dinder, Herefordshire, now ludicrously corrupted into "Oyster Hill." Towards the end of the campaign, in the autumn of A.D. 52, the battle which terminated the career of Caràdoc in the field was fought close to the confines of the Teme and the Clune in Shropshire. The Roman victory was complete. [10] The wife of Caràdoc and his daughter Gladys fell into the hands of the conquerors, and were conveyed to the castra at Urechean (Uriconium, Wrekin). Caràdoc himself took refuge, at her repeated solicitations, at Caer Evroc (York), with Arègwedd, or Aricia, the Cartismandua of Tacitus, queen of the Brigantes, and grand-niece of the infamous traitor in the Julian war, Mandubratius, or Avarwy. Here by her orders, with hereditary treachery, he was seized while asleep in her palace, loaded with fetters, and delivered to Ostorius Scapula. On intelligence of the event, Claudius ordered him and all the captive family to be sent to Rome. The British Triads commemorate this captivity of the royal Silurian family in their quaint fashion. "There were three royal families that were conducted to prison, from the great-great-grandfather to the great-grandchildren, without permitting one of them to escape. First the family of Llyr Llediaith, who were carried to prison at Rome by the Cesaridae...Not one or another of these escaped. They were the most complete incarcerations known as to families." The great-great-grandfather on this occasion was Llyr, the father of Bran, who subsequently died at Rome. Brân voluntarily surrendered himself as a hostage. The approach and arrival of Caràdoc at Rome are finely described by the ancient historians —

"Roma catenatum tremuit spectare Britannum." [11]

Since the days of Hannibal and Mithridrates, the only foe worthy the Roman arms entered the Eternal City amidst the excitement of three millions of inhabitants, who blocked up the line of the procession to obtain a view of the formidable and illustrious captive. The Senate was convened. The trial and speech of Caràdoc are familiar to every schoolboy. With an unaltered countenance, the hero of forty pitched fields, great in arms, greater in chains, took his position before the tribunal of the emperor, and thus delivered himself: — "Had my government in Britain been directed solely with a view to the preservation of my hereditary domains, or the aggrandizement of my own family, i might long since have entered this city an ally, not a prisoner; nor would you have disdained for a friend a king descended from illustrious ancestors, and the dictator of many nations. My present condition, stript of its former majesty, is as adverse to myself as it is a cause of triumph to you. What then? I was lord of men, horses, arms, wealth: what wonder if at your dictation I refused to resign them? Does it follow, that because the Romans aspire to universal dominion, every nation is to accept the vassalage they would impose? I am now in your power — betrayed, not conquered. Had I, like others, yielded without resistance, where would have been the name of Caràdoc? Where your glory? Oblivion would have buried both in the same tomb. Bid me live, I shall survive for ever in history one example at least of Roman clemency."

Such an address as this, worthy a king, a soldier, and a freeman, had never before been delivered in the Senate. Tacitus thought it worthy to be reported and immortalized by his pen. Its spirit reminded him of the old republican times of the Camilli, the Cincinnati, the Catones; a spirit long since extinct. The custom at those revolting displays of Roman pride and bloodthirstiness called "triumphs," was that at a certain spot on the Sacra Via the captive kings and generals should be removed from the procession, cast into the Tarpeian dungeons, to be there starved to death, strangled, or decapitated, and their dead bodies dragged by hooks into the Tiber. [12] Alas! for the chivalry of heathen warfare. The preservation of Caràdoc forms a solitary exception in the long catalogue of victims to this dastardly and nefarious policy; nor can it be accounted for, considering the inflexibility of Roman military usage, in any other way than by an immediate and supernatural intervention of Providence, which was leading by the hand to the very palace of the British king at Rome the great Apostle of the Gentiles. The family of Aulus Plautius, indeed, was already connected with that of Caràdoc, and an engagement existed between his daughter Gladys and Aulus Rufus Pudens Pudentinus, a young senator of large possessions in Samnium. But their united influences would never have sufficed to alter a fixed law of the Roman state in favour of an enemy that had tasked its utmost prowess and resources for so many years. The defeat at Caer Caràdoc and the betrayal of their sovereign had, moreover, served not to intimidate, but to infuriate and rouse to greater efforts, his subjects in Britain. The Silures elected his cousin Arviragus his successor in the pendràgonate. The Romans were beaten back across the Severn. Disaster followed disaster. Tacitus, loth to dilate on the misfortunes of the imperial arms, sums up the reverses of the war in a few expressive lines: — "In Britain, after the captivity of Caractacus, the Romans were repeatedly conquered and put to the rout by the single state of the Silures alone." [13] Perhaps this knowledge, that the execution of Caràdoc might still further imperil the Roman states in Britain, and the consideration that clemency might be the wisest policy towards a high-spirited and loyal enemy, dictated the course of Claudius. Be this as it may, the life of Caràdoc was spared, on condition of his never bearing arms against Rome again. A residence of seven years in free custody (*libera custodia*) at Rome was imposed upon him. His father Brân was accepted as one of the hostages, and he was allowed the full enjoyment of the revenues of the royal Silurian domains, forwarded to him by his subjects and council. Gladys, his daughter, was adopted by the Emperor Claudius, and assumed, of course, his family name — Claudia. Caràdoc took up his residence in the Palatium Britannicum, on the side of the Mons Sacer, converted afterwards by his grand-daughter, Claudia Pudentiana, into the first Christian Church at Rome, known first as the "Titulus," and now as St. Pudentiana. Here the nuptials of Claudia and Rufus Pudens Pudentinus were celebrated A.D. 53. Four children were the issue of this marriage — St. Timotheus, St. Novatus, St. Pudentiana, St. Praxedes. Of the sons of Caràdoc, Cyllinus and Cynon returned to Britain, the former succeeding on his death to the Silurian throne. The second, Lleyn, or Linus, remained with his father, and was, as we shall see subsequently, consecrated by St. Paul first bishop of the Roman Church.

Martial the epigrammatist was born A.D. 29: he went to Rome A.D. 49; he left Rome A.D. 86; and died at his native place, Bilbilis in Spain, A.D. 104, aged 75. As far as we can collect by collation, Claudia was born A.D. 36, and at her marriage with Rufus was in her 17th year. Martial was a familiar frequenter of the Pudentinian house, and in the habit of submitting his verses for emendations to its heir, Rufus. We have an epigram extant in which the witty but licentious poet complains of the severity of his young critic's castigations. It would have been well for his reputation, with no loss to his wit, had he allowed all his works to pass through the hands of Rufus before he had consigned them to the public ear. The epigram he addressed to the cousin of Rufus, Quintus Pomponius Rufus, then on military service in Dalmatia, on the nuptials of Claudia and Rufus, at which he appears to have been present, is subjoined. [14]

Four years afterwards, on the birth of Pudentiana, Martial addressed a second highly complimentary poem to the British princess, celebrating her beauty, grace, wit, and fascination. He represents her as uniting the separate accomplishments of the Roman and the Athenian ladies. Claudia, though the mother of three children, was only in her twenty-first year, and might with propriety be still termed "puella" by the poet. In the interval between the first and the present epigram, Pudens had been converted to Christianity, hence he is called Sancto Marito: —

"Claudia Ceruleis quum sit Rufina Britannis
   Edita quam Latiae pectora plebis habet!
Quale decus formae! Romanam credere matres
   Italidum possunt Attides esse suam
Die bene quod sancto peperit fcecunda marito
   Quod sperat generos quodque puella nurus
Sic placeat superis ut conjuge gaudeat una
   Et semper natis gaudeat ipsa tribus."

All the family of Caràdoc were attached to literary pursuits. Brân introduced the use of vellum into Britain from Rome; [15] and by the younger members copies of the best Roman authors were circulated in Siluria, and deposited in the principal receptacles of Druidic learning. Martial was no exception, and his verses appear to have become popular: —

"Dicitur et nostros cantare Britannia versus." — Lib. xi.

Claudia wrote several volumes of odes and hymns. Her aunt, Pomponia Graecina, received her *agnomen* from her intimate acquaintance with Greek literature. The palace, indeed, of the British king formed a focus and rendezvous, and perhaps the safest they could frequent, for the poets and authors of Rome. Nor did it cease to be so on his return to his native country; it continued to be the residence of Pudens and Claudia and their children. Some conception may be formed of its size and magnificence from the number of servants who constituted its ordinary establishment. These, as we learn from the Roman Martyrology, were two hundred males and the same number of females, all born on the hereditary estates of Pudens, in Umbria. [16]

The attachment between Pudens and Claudia first grew up when the former was stationed by Aulus Plautius as praetor castrorum at Regnum, now Chichester. We still possess in the Chichester Museum a remarkably interesting monument of the residence of Pudens in this city. Cogidunus, regulus of the Regni, was one of the kings included as allies — in fact, tributaries — under the Roman protectorate in the Claudian treaty of Colchester. Their native dynasties, laws, and lands were guaranteed to such states — the kings themselves becoming and being titled *Legati Augusti,* Lieutenants of the Roman emperor, as the heads of our counties are now styled Lieutenants of the Queen. They were bound to permit the construction of a Roman castra, garrisoned by Roman legionaries with their usual staff of engineers, in their chief city. The praetor of the castra held the military command within the allied territory. Such kings were considered and dealt with as traitors to the national cause by the Silurian and independent Britons, and their names either branded with the disgraceful stigma of *bradwr* (traitor), or consigned to oblivion by the Bardic chroniclers. Hence we find not a few commemorated in the pages of the Roman historians, of whose existence we can trace no vestige in the British. Of these Cogidunus is one. Tacitus remembered him, as he well might. For Tacitus was born A.D. 56, the year of the death of Claudius, and Cogidunus was alive A.D. 76, ten years after St. Paul's martyrdom, when Tacitus was in his twentieth year. In the year A.D. 1723, whilst excavating the foundations of some houses, the monument to which we refer, generally known as the Chichester stone, was discovered. The inscription, which was partly mutilated, and is cut in very bold characters, as restored by Horsley and Gale, is as follows: —

Neptuno et Minervae Templum

Pro Salute Domus Divine
Ex auctoritate tlb: claudii
Cogiduni Regis Legati Augusti in Britannia
Collegium Fabrorum et qui in eo
A Sacris sunt de suo dedicaverunt
Donante Aream Pudente Pudentini Filio.

"The College of Engineers, and ministers of religion attached to it, by permission of Tiberius Claudius Cogidunus, the king, legate of Augustus in Britain, have dedicated at their own expense, in honour of the divine family [the imperial family] this temple to Neptune and Minerva. The site was given by Pudens, son of Pudentinus."

Apart from its value in other respects, the inscription is interesting as evidence of the naturally pious bent of the young Roman commander's disposition, and, secondly, of the fact that to every legion in the Roman service was attached a staff of ministers of religion — a part of moral discipline in which these iron-minded heathens put to shame our own and other countries professing Christianity. The temple appears to have been erected about A.D. 50, before, of course, the conversion of Pudens or his marriage with Claudia.

We have now, A.D. 56, the royal Silurian family located at Rome on that part of the Mons Sacer called Scaurus, in the Palatium Britannicum, afterwards called the Titulus, or Hospitium Apostolorum, then St. Pudentiana, which name the building still retains. The minister of this church, and of the family of Pudens, was Hermas, mentioned by St. Paul, [17] surnamed, from his work bearing the title of *Pastor,* Hermas Pastor. The church was called also after him, Pastor. In front of this relic of eminent British and Apostolic times may still be seen, carved in characters corroded by age, the Latin inscription, attributed to the second century, of which the following is a translation: —

"In this sacred and most ancient of churches, known as that of Pastor, dedicated by Sanctus Pius Papa, formerly the house of Sanctus Pudens, the senator, and the home of the holy apostles, repose the remains of three thousand blessed martyrs, which Pudentiana and Praxedes, virgins of Christ, with their own hands interred." [18]

Baronius [19] has the following note upon the Titulus: — "It is delivered to us by the firm tradition of our forefathers that the house of Pudens was the first that entertained St. Peter at Rome, and that there the Christians assembling formed the Church, and that of all our churches the oldest is that which is called after the name of Pudens."

[1] Dion Cassius states that Caesar's original intention was to carry the war into the interior, but finding his forces inadequate to cope with the British in the field, he abruptly determined to close the campaign. (Lib. xxxix. p. 115, ed. 1606, fol.)

[2] The old belief that part of the Tower of London was built by Julius Caesar is known to every one; and the White Tower was pointed out as the part. "The White Tower" appears a version of the original British name Bryn Gwyn, but whether Caesar was lodged therein, or laid its foundation-stone, or was never at all entertained in London, there seems to us to be so much good sense in the sentiments put by Shakespeare on this point in the mouth of the young King Edward V, that we make no apology for transcribing them: —

"Prince Edward. Did Julius Caesar build the Tower, my lord?
Gloucester. He did. my gracious liege, begin that place; which since succeeding ages have re-edified.
Pr. Ed. Is it upon record, or else reported
   Successively from age to age he built it?
Glo. Upon record, my gracious lord.
Pr. Ed. But say, my lord, it were not registered;

> Methinks the truth should live from age to age,
> As 'twere entailed to all posterity,
> Even to the general all-ending day.
> *Glo.* So wise, so young!
> I say, without characters, fame lives long."
> *King Richard III,* act. iii, sc. 1.

[3] Aulus Gellius wrote an account of Caesar's invasion of Britain. He commemorates a British cry which seems to have produced a very lively impression on the Roman mind — "Horribilis ille Britannorum clamor, *Tori pen i Caisar*" ('Off with Caesar's head').

[4] "Hominum infinita multitudo" is Caesar's expression. Diodorus calls Britain πολυάνθρωπον νῆσον. In A.D. 110, Ptolemy enumerates fifty-six cities; later, Marcianus fifty-nine, πόλεις ἐπίσημους. British architects were in great demand on the Continent. "Redundabat Britannia artificibus," states Eumenius in his era.

[5] Tibullus. Horace implies that the Briton had scarcely been touched by Caesar's campaigns: —

"Intactus aut Britannus ut descenderet
    Sacra catenatus via."

In another Ode he writes, that nothing but the conquest of Britain was wanting to make Augustus "presens divus in terris," Od, lib. iii. 5.

[6] The accent in the British language is invariably on the penult — Caràdoc, Cynvèlin, Talièsin, Llewèlyn, &c. The Romans latinized Caràdoc by Caractacus, the Greeks hellenized it more correctly by Caratacos.

[7] "Camulo Deo Sancto et Fortissimo." — *Umbrian altar inscription.*

[8] "In Britannia circumdato a barbaris Vespasiano et in extreme-, periculo versante Titus Alius ejus patri metuens coronam hostium incredibili audacia disjecit." — *Suetonius in Vita Vespas.; Dion Cass.,* lib. ix.

[9] Taciti Annal., lib. ii. c. 24. The era of Tacitus was A.D. 80.

[10] Taciti Annal., lib. xii.

[11] ... "Rome trembled when she saw the Briton, though fast in chains."

[12] Jugurtha, king of Numidia, went mad during the procession, as he followed the car of his conqueror Marius.

[13] "In Britannia Romanos post Caractaci captivitatem ab unâ tantum Silurum civitate saepius victos et profligatos." — *Tac. Ann.,* lib. v. c. 28.

[14] "Claudia, Rufe, meo nubit Peregrina Pudenti:
    Macte esto taedis, O Hymenaee, tuis.
    Tarn bene rara suo miscentur cinnama nardo,
    Massica Theseis tarn bene vina cadis,
    Nec melius teneris junguntur vitibus ulmi,
    Nec plus Lotos aquas, littora myrtus amat.
    Candida perpetuo, reside, Concordia, lecto,
    Tamque pari semper sit Venus aequa jugo.
    Diligat ilia senem quondam: sed et ipsa marito,
    Tunc quoque quum fuerit, non videatur anus."

Lib. iv. p. 18.

[15] Coelbren, p. 25.

[16] Adjacent to the palace were baths on a corresponding scale, known subsequently as Thermae Timothinae and Thermae Novatianae. The palace baths and grounds were bequeathed by Timotheus to the Church at Rome. And these were the only buildings of any magnitude possessed by the Roman Church till the reign of Constantine. Hermas terms the Titulus "amplissima Pudentes domus." It was the *hospitium* for Christians from all parts of the world.
[17] Rom. xvi. 14.
[18] "In hac sanctâ antiquissima ecclesiâ," &c, &c. — *Baronius, ad Maii* 19.
[19] Annales Ecclesias, in Notis ad 19 Maii. Note on Pastor. Some authors affirm there were two distinct Hermas Pastors — one the above minister of the Titulus, so called because he belonged to the senatorian family of the name of Pastor; the second of later date, author of the treatise *Pastor,* and brother of Pius Papa. If this view is correct, both were ministers of the Titulus, for the letters of the latter from the Titulus to Timotheus in Britain are extant.

Vide also Moncaeus, Syntagma de Claudiâ Britannicâ, p. 18; Pastoris Epistolae ad Timotheum; Justini Martyris Apologia; Greek Menology, ad dies Pudentianas et Praxedis. That the palace of Claudia was the home of the apostles in Rome appears agreed upon by all ecclesiastical historians — even Robert Parsons, the Jesuit, admits it. "Claudia was the first hostess or harbourer both of St. Peter and St. Paul at the time of their coming to Rome." — *Parsons' Three Conversions of England,* vol. i. p. 16.

Chapter Three - The British Royal Family at Rome. — The Arimathaean, or First Introduction of Christianity into Britain

Having thus established the British king and his family in the Titulus, we turn our attention to St. Paul, who arrived at Rome for the first time on his appeal to Caesar, A.D. 58. [1]

A strong Christian Church, celebrated for its zeal and fidelity, existed in Rome before the visit of St. Paul or any other apostle to it. We know, from many passages in the Epistle to the Romans itself, that at the time of its composition and despatch St. Paul had not yet been to Rome. Amongst the members of the Church, however, were some not only of the most intimate fellow-labourers and friends, but relatives of the Apostle. Some of the latter, such as Andronicus and Junia, had been converted before him. Herodion is mentioned as another kinsman. In connection with Rufus Pudens who is saluted by name, occurs another salutation which originates an interesting question, the right solution of which would throw a flood of light on this part of the history both of Paul and Pudens — "Salute Rufus chosen in the Lord, and his mother and mine." Does this mean natural or spiritual relationship? We are inclined to believe the former. A spiritual father or mother is, in Gospel phraseology, the person who converts another to Christ. St. Paul's conversion was effected

by Christ Himself by a direct miracle. With respect to him the terms could not be applied to any human being. Was, then, the mother of Rufus the mother also of Paul? Were Rufus and Paul half-brothers — the latter, the elder, by a Hebrew, the former, the younger, by a second marriage with a Gentile, or proselyte Roman? This mother was a Christian, living with Rufus, and is termed also *his* mother by St. Paul. In the palace of Rufus, when at Rome, Paul spent most of his time, though he had also his own hired house. [2] The children of Claudia and Pudens, as we learn from the Roman Martyrologies, were brought up on his knees, and we find in the last scene of his life preceding his martyrdom, the only salutations sent by him to Timothy to be those of Eubulus, Claudia, Linus, and Pudens — the same family evidently ministering and attending to him to the last. There is, whichever way we decide, a closeness in the connection between the Apostle and the family of Pudens which has hitherto escaped observation, and remains to be explained. And this continued even after death, for the children of Pudens, all of whom suffered martyrdom, were interred by the side of the Apostle, as in a common family cemetery, in the Via Ostiensis. Leaving the question of the nature of this affinity in abeyance, we now observe —

1. That Pudens was converted before St. Paul came to Rome, and by some other Christian than Paul.

2. That Hermas Pastor appears at this very early date to have been the pastor at the Titulus, which constituted the place of meeting for the Gentile Church, or Church of the uncircumcision. The Hebrew Church, or Church of the circumcision, met at the House of Aquila and Priscilla. [3]

3. That the household of Aristobulus is greeted, but Aristobulus himself is not, being absent at the time from Rome. Hence arise the questions — Who were the evangelizers of the family of Claudia Britannica and Pudens? Where was Aristobulus absent? Was it in Britain? Was Britain evangelized in any degree before St. Paul came to Rome? and if so, by whom? — An investigation of the utmost interest.

The fairest way of treating the subject of the first introduction of Christianity into Britain seems to be to lay down an affirmative statement, adduce what evidence there is in support of it, and leave the reader to draw the conclusion whether it makes good such statement or not. We write as investigators, not as dogmatists, but our propositions must of necessity often assume the affirmative form, or we should be mere negationists of history.

Our statement, then, will take the following form: —

Christianity was first introduced into Britain by Joseph of Arimathasa, A.D. 36-39; followed by Simon Zelotes, the apostle; then by Aristobulus, the first bishop of the Britons; then by St. Paul. Its first converts were members of the royal family of Siluria — that is, Gladys, the sister of Caràdoc, Gladys (Claudia) and Eurgen his daughters, Linus his son, converted in Britain before they were carried into captivity to Rome; then Caràdoc, Brân, and the rest of the family, converted at Rome. The two cradles of Christianity in Britain were Ynys Wydrin, 'the Crystal Isle,' translated by the Saxons Glastonbury, in Somersetshire, where Joseph settled and taught, and Siluria, where the earliest churches and schools, next to Ynys Wydrin, were founded by the Silurian dynasty. Ynys Wydrin was also commonly known as Ynys Avàlon, and in Latin "Domus Dei," "Secretum Dei."

Now for the consecutive evidences of this statement. They have been collected at the cost of much research from various quarters, but the reader will remember that they are not presented as decisive. All historic evidence must be ruled by times and circumstances. If it be such as the times and circumstances of the era alone admit, it is entitled to be received in court, and if there is no contrary evidence which can be brought forward to cancel it, we must bring in, till such evidence be produced, a verdict of proven. The testimony in other historical cases may be stronger and more satisfactory, but we must be content in all cases to give judgment by such evidence as we can command. In ages when literature or written evidence had but very limited existence, tradition and general belief are the chief sources to which we can apply for the knowledge of broad facts, their details being a minor consideration.

The constant current of European tradition affirmed Britain to have been the first country in Europe which received the Gospel, and the British Church to be the most ancient of the Churches of Christ therein. The universality of this opinion is readily demonstrated.

I. Polydore Vergil in the reign of Henry VII, and after him Cardinal Pole (A.D. 1555), both rigid Roman Catholics, affirmed in Parliament, the latter in his address to Philip and Mary, that "Britain was the first of all countries to receive the Christian faith." "The glory of Britain," remarks Genebrard, "consists not only in this, that she was the first country which in a national capacity publicly professed herself Christian, but that she made this confession when the Roman empire itself was Pagan and a cruel persecutor of Christianity."

II. This priority of antiquity was only once questioned, and that on political grounds, by the ambassadors of France and Spain, at the Council of Pisa, A.D. 1417. The Council, however, affirmed it. The ambassadors appealed to the Council of Constance, A.D. 1419, which confirmed the decision of that of Pisa, which was a third time confirmed by the Council of

Sena, and then acquiesced in. This decision laid down that the Churches of France and Spain were bound to give way in the points of antiquity and precedency to the Church of Britain, which was founded by Joseph of Arimathaea "immediately after the passion of Christ." [4]

We may therefore accept as the general opinion of Christendom, the priority in point of antiquity over all others of the British Church. This opinion is well expressed by Sabellius: — "Christianity was privately confessed elsewhere, but the first nation that proclaimed it as their religion, and called itself Christian after the name of Christ, was Britain." [5]

It is certain that the primitive British, Irish, Scot, and Gallic Churches formed one Church, one communion, and that on the assumption of the Papacy, A.D. 606, by Rome, this great Celtic Church, which had been previously in full communion with primitive Rome, refused in the most peremptory terms to acknowledge her novel pretensions. It is, of course, this primitive British Church, and not the Roman Church introduced by Augustine, A.D. 596, into Kent among the Pagan Saxons, of which such priority must be understood. That such a Church existed on a national scale, and was thoroughly antagonistic to the Roman Church in its new form and usurpations in the person of Augustine, is so notorious, that we may dispense with all but a few testimonies in proof of the fact. "Britons," declares Bede, [6] "are contrary to the whole Roman world, and enemies to the Roman customs, not only in their Mass, but in their tonsure." The Britons refused to recognise Augustine, or to acquiesce in one of his demands. "We cannot," said the British bishops, "depart from our ancient customs without the consent and leave of our people." Laurentius, the successor of Augustine, speaks yet more bitterly of the antagonism of the Scottish Church: —

"We have found the Scotch bishops worse even than the British. Dagon, who lately came here, being a bishop of the Scots, refused so much as to eat at the same table, or sleep one night under the same roof with us." [7]

And the protest of the British Church itself, signed on its behalf by the Archbishop of St. David's, six bishops, and the abbot of Bangor, who conducted the conference with Augustine at Augustine's Oak, A.D. 607, place in still clearer light the gulf which the change of the primitive Roman Church into the Papacy formed between the Churches hitherto in full communion. It ran as follows: —

"Be it known and declared that we all, individually and collectively, are in all humility prepared to defer to the Church of God, and to the Bishop of Rome, and to every sincere and godly Christian, so far as to love every one according to his degree, in perfect charity, and to assist them all by word and in deed in becoming the children of God. But as for any other obedience, we know of none that he whom you term the Pope, or Bishop of Bishops, can demand. The deference we have mentioned we are ready to pay to him, as to every other Christian, but in all other respects our obedience is due to the jurisdiction of the Bishop of Caerleon, who is alone, under God, our ruler to keep us right in the way of salvation." [8]

It is plain from these and similar testimonies that Britain — 1. Was a distinct diocese of the empire. 2. That it was subject neither to the patriarch of Rome, nor to any foreign ecclesiastical jurisdiction. 3. That it had its sovereignty within itself. 4. That it never consulted the See of Rome nor any foreign power in its rites, discipline, government, or consecration of bishops and archbishops. 5. That it recognised no superior but God to its archbishop of Caerleon, or St. David. [9]

As late as the twelfth century no instance could be produced of the British metropolitan receiving the pall from Rome.

The two British metropolitans of London and York, Theon and Tediac, had retired from their Sees into Wales A.D. 586, ten years only before the arrival of Augustine.

In the Diocletian persecution the British Church supplied the following remarkable list of native martyrs: — Amphibalus. Bishop of LlandafT; Alban of Verulam; Aaron and Julius, presbyters of Caerleon; Socrates, Archbishop of York; Stephen, Archbishop of London; Augulius, his successor; Nicholas, Bishop of Penrhyn (Glasgow); Melior, Bishop of Carlisle, and above 10,000 communicants in different grades of society.

Its religious institutions were on an immense scale. William of Malmesbury describes the ruins of Bangor Iscoed Abbey in his days as those of a city — the most extensive he had seen in the kingdom. Two other British foundations in England retained their superiority over all others of a later date, under every change of rulers till the Reformation — St. Alban and Glastonbury. Of all the monasteries these continued the most popular and highly venerated. [10]

Tracing our course back from the Diocletian era, a *consensus* of authorities fixes the national establishment of Christianity in Britain somewhere about the middle of the second century. From A.D. 33, then, to A.D. 150, we have in round numbers a space of 120 years left for the propagation of the faith and the gradual conversion of the nation.

All accounts concur in stating that the person who baptized Lucius, or Lleeuer Mawr, the monarch who thus established the Church, was his uncle, St. Timotheus, the son of Pudens and Claudia, who was brought up on the knees of the apostles.

The infancy of Timotheus carries us back to Paul himself, to Claudia, to Pudens, to Linus, Caractacus, Bran, and the other members of the Silurian house in their captivity at Rome.

But we have seen that Pudens and others were Christians before Paul came to Rome, which carries the first British conversions to an earlier date than A.D. 58.

And thus we arrive within twenty-five years of the Crucifixion. In which of these years, then, was the Gospel first introduced into Britain?

Gildas, the British historian, who flourished A.D. 520 — 560, states expressly that it was introduced the last year of the reign of Tiberius Caesar. [11]

The Crucifixion took place in the seventeenth year of Tiberius. The last year of Tiberius would be his twenty-second. Consequently, if we follow Gildas, Christianity was introduced into Britain five years after the Crucifixion, that is, A.D. 38.

This is certainly an early period, but Gildas speaks positively — "ut scimus." It synchronizes with the first persecution of the Church by Saul of Tarsus, and its general dispersion. "They were all scattered abroad except the apostles." [12] If all, then Joseph of Arimathaea among them. Regarding Gildas' date as our starting-point, we have the following testimonies assigning the introduction of Christianity in or about the same year to Joseph of Arimathaea: —

1. Gregory of Tours, in the History of the Franks: [13] He flourished circiter A.D. 544 — 595. This is Gallic testimony.

2. The Pseudo-Gospel of Nicodemus, [14] supposed to be a composition of the fourth century. This is Oriental tradition.

3. Maelgwyn of Llandaff, the uncle of St. David. His era is circiter A.D. 450. His words being remarkable, we insert them at length: — "Joseph of Arimathaea, the noble decurion, received his everlasting rest with his eleven associates in the Isle of Avàlon. He lies in the southern angle of the bifurcated line of the Oratorium of the Adorable Virgin. He has with him the two white vessels of silver which were filled with the blood and the sweat of the great Prophet Jesus. [15]

This is British testimony, of one also personally acquainted with the interior of the church of Avàlon, or Domus Dei, and the exact spot within it of the restingplace of Joseph. The greater weight is due to Maelgwyn's evidence, as no fact is better established than the reconstruction of the Domus Dei on a cathedral scale by his nephew, St. David the Archbishop. [16]

4. The Vatican manuscript, quoted by Baronius in his "Ecclesiastical Annals," *ad annum* 35 (the same year in which the Acts of the Apostles state all, except the apostles, were scattered abroad from Judaea). The manuscript records that in this year Lazarus, Maria Magdalene, Martha, her handmaiden Marcella, Maximin a disciple, Joseph the Decurion of Arimathaea, against all of whom the Jewish people had special reasons of enmity, were exposed to the sea in a vessel without sails or oars. The vessel drifted finally to Marseilles, and they were saved. From Marseilles Joseph and his company passed into Britain, and after preaching the Gospel there, died. [17]

5. The *Chronicon* of Pseudo-Dexter, the *Fragmenta* of Haleca Archbishop of Saragossa, Freculphus and Forcatulus, [18] deliver the same statement professedly from primitive sources of unknown date. Cressy, Pitsaeus, Sanders, Alford, the Roman Catholic historians, concur with Gildas in the year, and with the above authorities in holding Joseph of Arimathaea to have been the first who preached Christ in Britain.

6. We possess abundant proofs that Britain was studded with Christian churches before the end of the second century, and whatever direction our investigations take, we find authorities unanimous in the statement that the church of Joseph in Avàlon, or Glastonbury, was the first and oldest of these churches, many affirming it to be the oldest or senior Christian church in the whole world. It will be useful to transcribe the conclusions arrived at by the historians who have treated on this subject before us.

"The church of Avàlon in Britain no other hands than those of the disciples of the Lord themselves built. — *Publius Discipulus.*

"The mother church of the British Isles is the Church in Insula Avallonia, called by the Saxons Glaston." — *Usher.*

"If credit be given to ancient authors, this church of Glastonbury is the senior church of the world." — *Fuller.*

"It is certain that Britain received the faith in the first age from the first sowers of the Word. Of all the churches whose origin I have investigated in Britain, the church of Glastonbury is the most ancient." — *Sir Henry Spelman.*

Had any doubt existed on this point of priority, it certainly would have been contested by some other church in our island, for it was not a question of mere chronology, but one which drew with it enormous privileges and advantages. It never was disputed. It was universally conceded: and upon it the long series of the royal charters of the church and monastery, from that of King Arthur, the nephew of its second founder, St. David, to that of Edward III, proceed. "The first church in the kingdom, built by the disciples of Christ," says the charter of Edgar. "This is the city," states the charter of Ina, or Ivor, "which was the fountain and origin of Christ's religion in Britain, built by Christ's disciples."

The tombs of Saxon and British kings, saints, bishops, and abbots, buried in and around its confines, confirm the charters.

Of the general truth of the Arimathaean mission there have been numerous supporters. No author, indeed, who has taken due pains to examine its evidences, rejects its main facts. "We dare not deny," writes the caustic Fuller, "the substance of the story." Bishop Godwin, in his quaint style, writes, "The testimonies of Joseph of Arimathaea's coming here are so many, so clear, and so pregnant, as an indifferent man cannot but discern there is something in it. [19] "Archbishop Usher defends it with his usual display of erudition, and with unusual vehemency of manner, as if the honour of ecclesiastical Britain rested on its truth. The reader will form his own judgment.

For our part, we cast aside the addenda and crescenda, the legends, poems, marvels which after ages, monk, troubadour, and historian piled high and gorgeously on the original foundation. That foundation must indeed have originally possessed no mean strength, depth, and solidity, to bear the immense superstructure which mediaeval superstition and literature emulated each other in erecting above the simple tomb of the Arimathaean senator in the Avàlon isle. This superstition was rising tide-high in the time of Augustine, A.D. 600. "In the western confines of Britain," he writes to the Pope, "there is a certain royal island of large extent, surrounded by water, abounding in all the beauties of nature and necessaries of life. In it the first neophytes of the catholic law, God beforehand acquainting them, found a Church constructed by no human art, but by the hands of Christ Himself, for the salvation of His people. The Almighty has made it manifest by many miracles and mysterious visitations that He continues to watch over it as sacred to Himself, and to Mary the mother of God." [20] The same edifice of figments has been built in all ages, more or less, on Christianity itself, but we do not therefore demur to the primitive facts of Christianity. Leaving details out of the question, the cardinal features of the first, or Arimathaean, mission of Christianity into Britain are, in our opinion, entitled to historic acceptance and registration.

These cardinal features we consider to be the following: — Joseph and his company, including Lazarus, Mary, Martha, Marcella, and Maximin, came at the invitation of certain Druids of high rank, [21] from Marseilles into Britain, *circiter* A.D. 38, 39; were located at Ynys Avàlon, the seat of a Druidic cor, which was subsequently made over to them in free gift by Arviragus. Here they built the first church, which became the centre and mother of Christianity in Britain. Here also they terminated their mortal career, the gentle and conciliatory character of Joseph securing the protection of the reigning family, and the conversion of many of its members. Joseph died and was interred A.D. 76.

The church was 60 ft. in length by 26 in breadth, built *Galileo more* of timber pillars and framework doubly wattled inside and out, and thatched with straw. [22] This simplicity might have been the effect of necessity or design. The Druidic faith required three essentials in every temple: — 1. It must be circular; 2. Hypaethral, or roofless at top, and open at the sides; 3. Its materials must be monoliths, vast single stones unhewed, untouched by metal. The Arimathaean church rose in direct though humble antagonism to the old Cyclopean architecture — it was oblong, it was of wood, it was roofed and covered in. The Druidic mind could not, without a strong effort, connect such a building with the ideas of religion and worship. It carried with it no image, no symbolism of the One, the Infinite, and the Darkless. The Briton on his way to one of the great cors — Amesbury or Stonehenge, with their miles of obelisks — would smile with pity on the *ecclesia,* or, as he rendered this new word from the East, the *eglwys* of the *Wyr Israel* (men of Israel). But the Druidic religion knew of no such monstrous abortions as intolerance and persecution. There is no instance of Druidism persecuting conscience or knowledge. Such crime was left for Rome, for a religion of foreign importation. Casting his eye round the circle of the horizon, and then upwards to the vast open dome of heaven, the Briton saw the outer ring, as it were, the circumference of his own Druidic cor; he would resume his march, trying to discover some possible identification in nature between an oblong pitched roof and the temple of the universe.

The tomb of Joseph was inscribed with the following epitaph, touching from its spirit of faith, peace, and humility: — [23]

[1] Jerome states St. Paul was sent to Rome in the second year of Nero, i.e. A.D. 56. in which date agree Bede, Ivo, Freculphus Platina, Scaliger, Capellus, Cave, Stillingfleet, Alford, Godwin *De Proesulibus,* Rapin, Bingham, Stanhope, Warner, Trapp. We believe this to be the true date, and its assumption would be more favourable to the tenor of this essay, as it would allow three years instead of one for the interview at Rome between St. Paul and Caractacus. We prefer, however, not to insist upon it.

[2] That the apostles having once been received into the Palatium Pudentinum, should continue to make it their home in Rome, is in conformity with our Lord's instructions, "Into whatsoever city or town ye enter, inquire who in it is worthy, and there abide till ye go thence." — Matthew x. n. At the same hospitium Justin Martyr was received. "Nobili revera atque prascipua in urbe Christi familia." — *Baron,* vol. i. p. 228.

[3] Rom. xvi. 5.

[4] "Statim post passionem Christi." An account of the pleadings at the Council of Constance will be found in a thin quarto, *Disceptatio super Dignitatem Anglioe et Gallioe in Concilio Constantiano,* Theod. Martin (Lovar. 1517).

Robert Parsons, the Jesuit, in his "Three Conversions of England," admits, in common with the great majority of Roman Catholic writers, that Christianity came into Britain direct from Jerusalem. "It seems nearest the truth that the British Church was originally planted by Grecian teachers, such as came from the East and not by Romans." — Vol. 1. p. 15. The Eastern usages of the British Church would alone attest the fact.

[5] Sabell. Enno., lib. vii. c. 5.

[6] Bede's Hist. Frag., quoted by Usher, "Ancient Irish Church," c. 4, Hist., lib. ii. c. 2. One demand of Augustine was that the British Church should recognise him as Archbishop. "At illi," says Bede, lib. ii. p. 112, "nihil horum se facturos neque ilium pro Archiepiscopo habituros esse respondebant." Bede must himself, one would suppose, from his own testimony in favour of the British Church, and his knowledge of its extent and institutions, have felt some astonishment at this de-

mand of an emissary whose only religious establishment in Britain was a solitary church among the Pagans of Kent. "The Britons," he writes, lib. i. c. 4, "preserved the faith which they had received under King Lucius uncorrupted and entire in peace and tranquillity, until the time of the Emperor Diocletian." Nicholas Trivet says, "Abbot Dinothus, of Bangor, treated Augustine with contempt."

[7] Laurentii Epist. ad Papam; Bede, Eccles. Hist., ii. c. 4.

[8] Hengwrt MSS.; Humphry Llwyd; Sebright MSS.; Cottonian Library (British Museum), Cleopatra, E. i. 1.

[9] Spelmanni Concilia; Sir Roger Twysden, Historical Vindication; Brerewood, p. 113; Collier, vol. 1. p. 6, &c; Bishop Lloyd's Government, &c, &c.

[10] It is certain, states Spelman (p. 18), that the people of that province held no oath so sacred as that "by the old church" (Glastonbury), fearing nothing so much as to incur the guilt of perjury in taking it. "The church of Glastonbury, from its antiquity called by the -Angles' Ealde Churche,' savoured of sanctity from its very foundation. Here arrive whole tribes of the lower orders, thronging every path. Here, divested of their pomp, assemble the opulent. It has become the crowded residence of the literary and religious. There is no corner of the church in which the ashes of some saint do not repose. The very floor inlaid with polished stones, and the sides of the altar, and even the altar itself, above and beneath, are laden with the multitude of relics. The antiquity, and multitude of saints, have endowed the place with such sanctity that at night scarcely any one presumes to keep vigil there, or during the day to spit upon the floor. St. Patrick is buried by the right side of the altar in the 'old church.' The men of Ireland frequent it to kiss the relics. St. David, that celebrated and incomparable man, built and dedicated the second church here. He sleeps by St. Patrick." — *William of Malmesbury*, b. i. c. 2. St. Aidan was buried by the side of St. David.

[11] "We know that Christ, the true Son, afforded His light to our island in the last year of Tiberius Caesaris." — *Histor. Briton.* Usher terms Gildas "auctor veracissimus."

[12] Acts viii. 1.

[13] p. 133.

[14] Ad finem.

[15] "Joseph ab Arimathea nobilis decurio in insula Avallonia cum xi. Sociis suis somnum cepit perpetuum et jacet in meridiano angulo lineae bifurcatas Oratorii Adorandae Virginis. Habit enim secum duovascula argentea alba cruore et sudore magni prophetas Jesu perimpleta." — Thick vellum Cottonian MS., quoted also by Usher, *Melchini Fragmentum.* Joseph of Arimathaea is by Eastern tradition said to have been the younger brother of the father of the Virgin Mary. The records of Glastonbury, as cited by Malmesbury and others, preserved the genealogy of his descendants in Britain: — "Helias nepos Joseph genuit Josua, Josua genuit Amminadab, Amminadab Castellor," &c. — *Historia de Glastonbury.*

[16] In the two "vascula argentea alba," full of the Saviour's blood and sweat shed on the cross and at Gethsemane, we have the first nucleus of the celebrated legend and a quest of the SantGreal. They gave the name of the Crystal Isle to Glastonbury. The Britons commemorate (writes Forcatulus) that Joseph brought with him the pledge and testimony of the sacred Eucharist, namely, the chalice which was used by the Saviour, and placed before His most holy guests the apos-

tles, and which is preserved by them (the Britons) as the pledge of the safety of Britain, as the palladium was of that of Troy. — *Fortaculus de Gallor. Imperio et Philos.*, lib. vii. p. 989. Greal in British is a collection of elements; *Sant-Greal*, the holy elements.

[17] The respective dates of A.D. 35 and 38 allow three years between the expulsion of Joseph from Judaea and his settlement in Britain — an undesigned harmony which goes far chronologically to confirm the common record.

[18] Lib. vii. p. 989.

[19] Godwin's "Catalogue of Bishops," Praesul., p. 11.

[20] Epistolae ad Gregorium Papam.

[21] "Negotium habuit cum Druidis quorum primi precipuique doctores erant in Britannia." — *Freculphus, apud God.*, p. 10.

[22] And such also was the primitive Capitol of Rome: —
"Quae fuerat nostri si quaeras Regia nati,
   Adspice de Canna straminibusque Domum."
      Ovid, Faest. ad Fest. Roma.

[23] Hearne's Antiquities of Glastonbury; Leland, ibid.; John of Tynemouth, Ad Josephum Arimath.

"Ad Britannos veni post Christum Sepelivi. Docui. Quievi."

Of the perpetual exemption of the twelve ploughs of land conferred by Arviragus on the Arimathsean Church, the Domesday Survey of A.D. 1088 supplies curious confirmation. "The Domus Dei, in the great monastery of Glastingbury, called the Secret of the Lord. This Glastingbury church possesses, in its own villa, xii. hides of land which have never paid tax." [1]

After A.D. 35 — 36 Joseph disappears from the Scripture narrative.

The Greek and Roman menologies and Martyrologies commemorate with scrupulous jealousy the obituaries and death-places of all the earlier Christian characters of mark who died within the pale of the Roman empire. They nowhere record those of Joseph. Now we know from Tertullian that Britain was Christian before it was Roman. The Dove conquered where the Eagle could make no progress. "Regions in Britain which have never been penetrated by the Roman arms," are his words (A.D. 192) "have received the religion of Christ." If this statement were correct, after the war between Rome and Britain had raged for a century and a half, from A.D. 43 to A.D. 192 — and in a national point of view it is impartial testimony, for Tertullian was an African — it is obvious that the Arimathasan mission must have been founded in the heart of independent Britain, quite out of the pale, therefore, of the Roman empire. And this inference tallies with the rest of the evidence. Joseph died in these *loca inaccessa Romanis*. His death, therefore, could not be chronicled by Greek or Roman Churches.

Lazarus is asserted to have accompanied Joseph. The only record we possess of him beyond the Scripture narrative [2] is in a very ancient British Triad: "The Triad of Lazarus, the three counsels of Lazarus: Believe in God who made thee; Love God who saved thee; Fear God who will judge thee." [3] It is difficult to explain how the name and counsel of Lazarus could find their way into these peculiarly British memorials except by his presence and teaching in Britain.

Finally, were there any other eminent converts, besides those of the Silurian family, made at this very early date in Britain? Three are particularly mentioned — Beatus, whose first name was Suetonius, Mansuetus, and Marcellus.

Beatus, born of noble parents in Britain, was there also converted and baptized. He became the founder of the Helvetian Church. He fixed his mission at Underseven, on the lake of Thun, disposing of all his property to ransom prisoners of war. His death occurred in the cell still shown at Underseven, A.D. 96 [4]

Mansuetus, born in Hibernia, converted and baptized in Britain, was sent afterwards from Rome with St. Clement, afterwards the second bishop of Rome, to preach the Gospel in Gaul. He founded the Lotharingian Church, fixing his mission at Toul, where, after extending his labours to Illyria, he suffered martyrdom, A.D. 110. [5]

Marcellus, a noble Briton, became bishop of Tongres, and afterwards founder-bishop of Treves — the diocese which for centuries exercised the chief influence in the Gallic Church. The conversion of Linus, the son of Caractacus, is attributed to him. [6]

Before, therefore, the incorporation of Britain with the Roman empire, whilst the war of invasion raged, we have before us these remarkable facts: — 1. A young and vigorous Christian Church, direct from Jerusalem and the East, and which had never touched or passed through Rome, was in full and successful work in the heart of independent Britain, under the protection of the very sovereign and family that conducted the war against Rome. 2. This native Church, though so young, does not limit its operations to Britain. It ramifies from Britain to the Continent, and becomes, through native-born missionaries, the mother-Church of Gaul, Lotharingia, and Helvetia. Providence, for the most part, works in a very noiseless way, by natural means. Nothing could be more natural than that Joseph and his companions — for whom, as Christians, there was neither peace nor safety among their own countrymen; for whom, as Christians and Jews, there was no assurance of their lives in any Roman province — should seek refuge in the only independent kingdom of the West, whose national religion, like their own, was marked for destruction on the Continent; for, as we have seen, the decrees of Augustus, Tiberius, and Claudius constituted Druidism a capital offence. [7] Nothing could be more natural than that Guiderius and Aviragus, on the intercession of influential Druids, should receive and protect such refugees, and in accordance with their own Druidic principles, leave whatever religion they professed to the voluntary acceptance or rejection of their subjects. All this, we repeat, was very natural, yet we may well affirm that Providence was working in the wheel of Nature. If the stoker was Nature, the engineer was Providence. Under this reflection lies another. Whatever the errors of Druidism were, it was, in its main truths, a grand religion, forming grand and truthful characters. Its foundation-maxim was, "Truth against the world" literally, against "all being." [8]

Now, if we just cast one eye on Britain, on a Druidic Caractacus, Arviragus, or Claudia, listening from their thrones to a Christian missionary, because he professed to bring and to preach truth, and Christ as the Truth, the Way, and the Life; then cast the other on a Pilate, asking, in the profoundest disbelief in all virtue and goodness, "What is truth?" we shall see at a glance that Britain was prepared, and the Roman empire not prepared, for Christianity. The British and Roman minds were different. Druidism, therefore, dissolved by the natural action of its own principles into Christianity. No persecution until the tenth, under Diocletian, touched Britain, for Christianity had become nationality. And the Diocletian was stopped in two years, on his own responsibility, at the hazard of civil war, by Constantius. Then rose Constantine, with a British army sworn to put down the persecution of Christianity for ever. The clue is a national, a British one.

The next missionary after Joseph was Simon Zelotes the apostle. There can be little doubt, we think, on this point. One Menology assigns the martyrdom of Zelotes to Persis in Asia, but others agree in stating he suffered in Britain. Of these the principal authority is Dorotheus, Bishop of Tyre, in the reigns of Diocletian and Constantius (A.D. 300). His testimony we consider decisive: — "Simon Zelotes traversed all Mauritania, and the regions of the Africans, preaching Christ. He was at last crucified, slain, and buried in Britain." [9] Crucifixion was a Roman penalty for runagate slaves, deserters, and rebels: it was not known to the British laws. We conclude Simon Zelotes suffered in the east of Britain, perhaps, as tradition affirms, in the vicinity of Caistor, under the prefecture of Caius Decius, the officer whose atrocities were the immediate cause of the Boadicean war. Two things strike the investigator of early Christian history: the marvellous manner in which Christian seed is found growing and fructifying in unheard-of places; the indifference of the sowers to perpetuating their own name and labours. They seem to have been quite satisfied and blest in sowing Christ, and then resting. The epitaph of Joseph of Avàlon would express the feelings of all: — *Docui, Quievi*, 'I taught, I have entered on my rest.' Beautiful as is this in fact and faith, it is very unsatisfactory in history. As Christians we feel its propriety; as writers we desiderate more of that yearning for immortality on earth which inspires the Greek and Latin authors, and inspires us also in reading them. Yet the effects of the Christian principle are undoubtedly greater; for the principle it is which meets us face to face. It is Christ or self. We come on a field: the sower has inclosed it, built round it strongly, sowed proved seed in it, entrusted it to a few like-minded men, and he vanishes. He is crucified a thousand miles off, leaves no memoir of himself, no message to posterity, no foot-mark on the geology of the Church. In perusing the Apostolic Epistles we are struck by the maximum of censure, the minimum of approval conveyed to the Churches. We are apt to think they had little force or vitality. But when we extend our survey to the whole empire of Rome, we are almost terrified at the subterraneous shocks with which these Churches are everywhere bringing Pagan temple and tower to the ground. We try to calculate and value this power. We fail in doing it. The Roman government failed also. It is an unknown power, the source of which is from above.

3. Next to Joseph and Simon Zelotes came Aristobulus. "It is perfectly certain," writes Alford, [10] "that before St. Paul had come to Rome Aristobulus was absent in Britain." We have seen he was not at Rome when Paul wrote his Epistle. Now Aristobulus must have been far advanced in years, for he was the father-in-law of St. Peter. His wife was the subject of the miracle recorded by St. Matthew. His daughter bore Peter a son and a daughter. We have the following evidences that he preached the Gospel and was martyred in Britain: —

The Martyrologies of the Greek Churches: — "Aristobulus was one of the seventy disciples, and a follower of St. Paul the Apostle, along with whom he preached the Gospel to the whole world, and ministered to him. He was chosen by St. Paul to be the missionary bishop to the land of Britain, inhabited by a very warlike and fierce race. By them he was often scourged, and repeatedly dragged as a criminal through their towns, yet he converted many of them to Christianity. He was there martyred, after he had built churches and ordained deacons and priests for the island." [11]

Haleca, Bishop of Augusta, to the same effect: — "The memory of many martyrs is celebrated by the Britons, especially that of St. Aristobulus, one of the seventy disciples." [12]

Dorotheus, A.D. 303: — "Aristobulus, who is mentioned by the Apostle in his Epistle to the Romans, was made bishop in Britain." [13]

Adonis Martyrologia: — "Natal day of Aristobulus, Bishop of Britain, brother of St. Barnabas the Apostle, by whom he was ordained bishop. He was sent to Britain, where, after preaching the truth of Christ and forming a Church, he received martyrdom." [14]

The British Achau, or Genealogies of the Saints of Britain: — "These came with Brân the Blessed from Rome to Britain — Arwystli Hên (*Senex*), Hid, Cyndaw, men of Israel; Maw, or Manaw, son of Arwystli Hên." [15]

According to the genius of the British tongue, Aristobulus becomes Arwystli.

A district in Montgomeryshire, on the Severn, perpetuates by its name (Arwystli) the scene of his martyrdom.

The Britons must have had Arwystli in person among them; they must have been struck by the age of the venerable missionary, or the epithet *Senex* would not have become amongst them part of his name.

There are several points here to be noted. The first is, that Aristobulus was sent into Britain by St. Paul before St. Paul came himself to Rome, and even before the Epistle to the Romans was written, for Aristobulus, when St. Paul wrote it, had left for his mission. The large space given by the Roman historians to the wars in Britain demonstrates the interest felt in them by the whole empire. Britain was a familiar term in every household. Upon it the whole military attention had for some years been concentrated. The name of Arviragus had by this time attained as great a celebrity as that of his cousin Caractacus — it was in every one's mouth; and Juvenal could suggest no news which would have been hailed by the Roman people with more intense satisfaction than that of his fall:—

> "Hath our great enemy
> Arviragus, the car-borne British king,
> Dropped from his battle-throne?"

It is certain, therefore, that St. Paul, who travelled everywhere, mixing with every kind of society, must have been as well acquainted with Britain, and the events passing therein, as any other intelligent Roman citizen. There was everything to attract his eye to it as a field for Gospel labour and enterprise.

But have we any Scripture evidence that St. Paul at this time thought at all of Western Europe? Undoubtedly we have. Commentators and writers of his life generally refer to his visit to Spain as contemplated after his first imprisonment at Rome. A reference to the passage in the fifteenth chapter of the Epistle shows, on the contrary, that his journey to Spain was meditated not only before he came to Rome, but that it was his principal object in leaving the East, his call at Rome being simply on the way. "Whensoever I take my journey into Spain, I will come to you, for I trust to see you on my journey, and to be brought on my way thitherward by yo?" [16] He speaks of the journey as a thing decided upon, taking Rome by the way. Literally, in the original it is, "I hope in passing through to see you." It was the West of Europe, then, beyond Rome, not Rome itself, which was the Apostle's mark, even at this comparatively early date. All the incidents and delays which occurred between this date (A.D. 56), and the termination of his first imprisonment at Rome, were interruptions of his original plan of operations. His destination was the extreme West, and this was in accordance with the command of Christ, "I will send thee tar hence to the Gentiles." According to the Scriptures, therefore, and the view we have therein of Paul's own mind, we think we are justified in concluding that having already sent Aristobulus into Britain, he intended to traverse Spain himself, and thence join his fellow-labourer in our island; for it is plain that Aristobulus acted as wholly under Paul's instructions in Britain as Titus in Crete or Timothy in Asia Minor. "He preached the Gospel with St. Paul to the whole world, and ministered to him." [17]

It appears that Brân left Rome with Aristobulus, his son Manaw, Hid, and Cyndaw, before Caràdoc. He was accompanied also by Eurgain, the eldest daughter of Caràdoc, and her husband Salog, lord in her right of Caer Salog (Salisbury), a Roman patrician. Hid established his mission under the protection of Bran, his grandson Cyllinus (eldest son of Caràdoc), Salog and Eurgain, in the centre of Siluria, on the spot in Glamorganshire known from that period till the present as Llan-Ilid. At this *Llan*, or 'consecrated inclosure,' the Princess Eurgain founded and endowed the first Christian cor, or choir, in Britain. From this Cor-Eurgain issued many of the most eminent teachers and missionaries of Christianity down to the tenth century. Of the saints of this cor, from Hid in succession, there are catalogues in the "Genealogies of the Saints of Britain." [18]

Eastern and Western testimonies concur in thus proving the Aristobulian mission to Britain under the Sanction of Brân and his family. We complete the chain with the two following, from historic sources: —

"The three blessed sovereigns of the isle of Britain: — 1. Brân, son of Llyr Llediaith, who first brought the faith of Christ to the Cymry from Rome, where he had been seven years a hostage for his son Caràdoc, whom the Romans put in prison, after being betrayed by the plotting, deceit and enticement of Arèddig. 2. Lleuver, or Leirwig (Lucius), son of Coel, son of St. Cyllin, son of Caràdoc, son of Brân, son of Llyr Llediaith, called Lleuver the Great, who founded the first church of Llandaff, and first gave the privileges of the country and nation to all who professed the faith in Christ. 3. Cadwalladr the Blessed, who gave protection within all his lands to the Christians who fled from the pagan Saxons who wished to slay them." [19]

"The three priorities of the Cymry: — 1. Priority as the first colonizers of Britain; 2. Priority of government and civilization; 3. Priority as the first Christians of Britain." [20]

In an ancient collection of British proverbs we find certain sayings transmitted of Brân and the first Christians of Britain: —

"Hast thou heard the saying of Hid,
The saint of the race of Israel?
'No folly but ends in misery.'

Hast thou heard the saying of the noble Bran,
The blessed, to all the renowned?
'There is no good but God Himself.'

Hast thou heard the saying of Caràdoc,
The exalted son of the noble Brân?
'Oppression persisted in brings on death.'"

We have at this stage of the inquiry two distinct cradles of Christianity in Britain — the mission of Joseph in Avàlon, and the Cor-Eurgain at Llan-Ilid in Wales; the former protected by Arviragus, the latter fostered by the family of Caràdoc, his cousin. We can entertain no reasonable doubt that very intimate ties bound these two Christian missions together. St. Barnabas, Aristobulus his brother, and Joseph were members of the Jerusalem Church — they were of the one hundred and twenty which constituted it prior to the day of Pentecost — the same spiritual union, the same friendship, the same one faith, one heart, one mind, one baptism, one hope, one Lord, would joint them together in Britain as in Jerusalem. Both establishments were out of the pale of Rome, both among the free states of Britain. Beyond Siluria, among the Ordovices, the protection of Brân did not avail Aristobulus: Joseph came direct from Jerusalem, and was therefore regarded with favour; Aristobulus came from Rome, from the metropolis of the national enemy, and fell, perhaps, rather a victim to this fact than a martyr to religion. In Siluria itself the royal family were hard pressed to reconcile their subjects to the presence of men in any way, however slightly, connected with Rome, so unappeasable was the hatred borne to the invaders, so easily misapprehended and confounded every embassage from their city. Every overture of peace made by the Roman government to this *ferox provincia* was sternly rejected; rigour and mildness were alike thrown away. "The race of the Silures," observes Tacitus, "was not to be changed by clemency or severity." [21] Even after the treaty which incorporated Britain with Rome (A.D. 118), two-thirds of the whole military force of the island continued to be stationed on the frontiers of Wales, at Chester and Caeleon. The same dogged opposition to the foreigner characterised the same race in the West in the later Saxon eras. "It is certain," writes Kemble, "that neither Roman nor Saxon produced any effect worth mentioning on the Cymric race and language west of the Severn. We see indeed what little effect all the centuries since then, though but a river divides the two races, has produced upon the British language." [22]

Great caution, therefore, was called for in the exercise, under these circumstances, of the royal protection. Meanwhile, however, the cor continued to strike roots. The royal family themselves remained firm in the profession of Christianity. Cyllinus, who acted as regent in the absence of his father Caràdoc, had all his children baptized. Converts increased, and more teachers arrived from Greece and Rome. The following notice of St. Cyllinus is extracted from the family records of Jestyn ap Gwrgant, Prince of Glamorgan, in the eleventh century: —

"Cyllin ab Caràdog, a wise and just king. In his days many of the Cymry embraced the faith in Christ through the teaching of the saints of Cor-Eurgain, and many godly men from the countries of Greece and Rome were in Cambria. He first of the Cymry gave infants names; for before, names were not given except to adults, and then from something characteristic in their bodies, minds, or manners." [23]

[1] "Domus Dei in magno Glaston. monasterio quod secretum Domini vocatur, Ecclesia Glaston. habet in ipsa villa xii. hydas quae nunquam geldaverunt." — *Domesday Survey*, fol., p. 449.
[2] The tradition of the Church of Lyons makes him return with Martha and Mary to Marseilles, of which town he became the first bishop, and there died.
[3] Triads of Primitive Britain.
[4] Theatr. Magn. Britan., lib. vi. p. 9.
[5] Pantaleon, De Viris Illus. Germaniae, pars. I.; Guliel. Eisengren, cent. 2, p. 5; Petrus Mersaeus, De Sanctis German.; Franciscus Guilliman, Helvetiorum Historia, lib. i. c. 15; Petrus de Natalibus, Episcop. Regal. Tallensis.
[6] Marcellus Britannus, Tungrorum episcopus postea Trevirorum Archiepiscopus," &c. — *Mersaeus, De Archiepiscopis Trevirensium.*
[7] "Penitus religionem Druidarum abolevit Claudius." — *Suetonius, in Vitâ Claud.*
[8] St. Paul's maxim, "We can do nothing against the truth," breathes a kindred spirit, and would at once conciliate a Druidic hearer.
[9] Dorotheus, Synod, de Apostol.; Synopsis ad Sim Zelot.
[10] Alford's Regia Fides, vol. 1. p. 83. Alford. whose proper name was Griffiths, and who assumed the name of Alford on entering the Society of Jesuits, is, next to Baronius, the most learned of the Roman Catholic historians. His *Regia Fides* is a wonderful monument of erudition and research.
[11] Greek Men., ad 15 March.
[12] Halecae Fragmenta in Martyr.
[13] Synopsis ad Aristobulum.
[14] In Diem Martii 17.
[15] Achau Saint Prydain.
[16] Rom. xv. 24.

[17] Greek Menology, ad Diem Martii 17.
[18] Achau Saint Prydain. In these *Achau,* or genealogies, Eurgain is commemorated as the first female saint of the isle of Britain. Her conversion., therefore, preceded that of her sister Claudia. Hid was a Hebrew: —
  "Hast thou heard the saying of Ilid,
    One come of the race of Israel?
  'There is no mania like passion.'" —
British Proverbs.
[19] Triads of the isle of Britain.
[20] Triads of the Cymry.
[21] "Silurum gens non atrocitate, non dementia mutabatur" — *Taciti Annal,* lib. ii. c. 24.
[22] History of the Anglo-Saxons, vol. 1. Tacitus, in his Life of Agricola (c. 21), takes occasion to notice the stubborn attachment of the Briton to his native tongue. And it is one of the most remarkable facts connected with the occupation of Britain by the Romans, that though they entirely recast the languages of the Continent through the medium of their own, they did not leave probably a hundred Latin words behind them in Britain: within twenty years of their departure Latin had ceased to be spoken in the island.
[23] Gwehelyth Iestyn ap Gwrgant.

Nero

Nero had succeeded Claudius Sept. 28, A.D. 53. He was in his seventeenth year, and for some time remained under the influence of Seneca, a Stoic philosopher in profession but in practice a grinding usurer. The capital of this minister amounted to fifteen million pounds sterling of modern money. Two millions of this he advanced to the Iceni of Britain on the security of their public buildings. We doubt if Rothschild or any modern capitalist would advance half the sum on such buildings as may now be found in the old Icenic counties. The king of the Iceni was Prasutagus, his queen Victoria (in British, Vuddig or Boeddig — Boadicea). Tacitus speaks of him as a sovereign whose wealth was notorious at Rome — *longâ clarus opulentiâ.*

The commerce between Britain and the Continent continued to be vigorously conducted. Tacitus informs us that the great foreign emporium was London, a city the foundation of which the British annals carried back 270 years before that of Rome, i.e. B.C. 1020. [1] Above 80,000 Roman citizens, according to the Roman historians, perished in the Boadicean war, of whom the greater number resided in London. A Roman garrison stationed in the Praetorium — which extended along the Thames from the temple of Diana, where now stands St. Paul's, to the Bryn Gwyn, or White Mount, the site of the Tower — protected their property and interests. It was just as easy for an apostle to find his way into Britain as for any of these 80,000, amongst whom there must have been a fair proportion of Christians. The Roman citizen could travel from Babylon to London along the great military itinera of the empire, more slowly indeed, but with fewer civil inconveniences in the shape of passports and stoppages, and no less security, than an Englishman can now. It was not in mediaeval Europe, divided amongst a thousand independent marauding states and barons, nor in the pathless wilds of a new world, but over the length and breadth of an empire possessed of a system of roads laid down with consummate engineering skill, and remaining, until the invention of railroads, without rivals on a great scale, that the first preachers of the Gospel had to travel. The Roman *iter* at Babylon would conduct them, under the protection of one law, one government, without a frontier, to Calais. The whole empire was a network of connected arteries, along which a traveller might take his ease from anywhere to anywhere under the overshadowing protection of the Eagles of the Caesars. It was not till he had crossed the British Channel that the din and terror of war assaulted his senses. So profound, indeed, until the brief civil commotion that resulted in placing the Vespasian family on the throne, was the peace which prevailed through Europe, that the Roman annalists are driven, for lack of national events, to fill page after page with court scandals, with the personal debaucheries and cruelties of the emperors. These emperors were despots created by the democracy against the oligarchy; they held the same position as the Tudors of later times in Britain. When a noble raised his head above his fellows, like Tarquin and the poppies, they cut it remorselessly and unscrupulously down. A lover of the old oligarchic times, such as Tacitus, would — and no doubt in many cases justly stigmatize such executions as judicial murders, and transmit their authors to the execration of posterity. The people at large were unaffected; the lightning passed over them; and, in return, it was the dagger of the oligarch in the chamber, not the popular tumult, which the Caesar dreaded. He walked the streets a simple citizen without guards, but he went to the Senate armed. Meanwhile, Ostorius Scapula in Britain suffered a defeat from Arviragus at Caervèlin, near Caerleon. Exhausted in mind and body by the harassing vicissitudes of the war, he petitioned to be recalled. He was succeeded by Didius Gallus, who founded Cardiff, still called by the Welsh *Caer Dydd*, 'the Castle of Didius.' After a short command Didius gave way to Veranius, under whom the Roman armies were again driven behind the Plautian line of fortresses, and their headquarters fixed at Verulam. Veranius was superseded by Suetonius Paulinus, a second Fabius Cunctator, and regarded as the ablest tactitian in the Roman service. [2] He had under him the ninth, fourteenth, twentieth (Vicesima Valens Victrix), and second (Augusta) legions.

The expression of Tacitus, that Britain had long been the field for the employment of the great generals and picked armies of the empire, [3] may be readily understood by merely reading over the names of the Roman commanders who were successively entrusted with the conduct of war — Aulus Plautius, Geta, Vespasian and Titus, Ostorius Scapula, Suetonius Paulinus, Cerealis, Julius Frontinus, Julius Agricola, Sallustius, Lucullus, under whom the island was lost, and the Roman armies a second time withdrawn to the Continent, A.D. 86; from which time till A.D. 118 we have but one solitary Roman name occurring in British history, Neratius Marcellus. From A.D. 43 to A.D. 86 sixty pitched battles were fought. "The series of invasions and sanguinary conflicts," observes Smith in his "Ancient Religions," [4] "between the Romans and Britons have no parallel in any age or country." "We are able to perceive," writes Richardson, "from the partial story furnished by the invaders themselves, that conquest was never more dearly attempted than in the case of Britain by the Romans. By no people was every inch of country at any age contested with more bravery and surrendered more stubbornly than by the aboriginal fathers of this isle. They had become a very populous nation, so versed in military tactics as to meet the armies, which had been carrying the Roman banners over the most famed and intellectual quarters of the world, on such formidable terms, as to render victory at every encounter little better than defeat. They had settled laws and institutions, were distinguished for an ardent love of liberty, in defence of which the highest degree of valour and self-devotion were on all occasions manifested. It is certain they reverenced the laws by which they had been long governed, and evinced profound homage for the memory of their forefathers: nor can we less credit their undaunted energy against the mercenary and implacable plunderers of the world, against whose experienced arms they had to contend. A man must be a barbarian himself to suppose that such a nation could be barbarous. The idea is simply ludicrous." [5]

This firm resistance to the Roman arms was mainly due to the national religion — to Druidism, which acted then much the same as Protestantism did on the British mind in the popish invasion of the Armada. Druidism had been persecuted by pagan Rome on the Continent as Protestantism in the Tudor era was by papal Rome: both had their headquarters and stronghold in Britain, both had common points admirably suited to the native bent and genius of the British race; both were religions of freedom; and both were thoroughly identified with British independence and grandeur. The Druid, indeed, regarded the Roman mythologic religion with much the same mixture of contempt and hatred that a strong Protestant does still the image system and inquisition practices of the Papacy. "When the Romans," observes Cleland, "effected a footing in Britain, they found in Druidism a constant and implacable enemy to their usurpation. They would have been glad to introduce their religion, but to that point there was an invincible obstacle in the horror and contempt of the natives for a religion formed by a corruption of their own allegories; which made the name of their heathen gods as familiar to them as Julius Caesar states, but in a sense which excluded them from reception in a divine one." [6]

The Briton soon perceived the fact that Christianity and Druidism were the two religions persecuted by Rome. The gathering prejudice against the former, because the Aristobulean mission came from Rome, gave way to strong predilections in its favour. A large class of Britons, it is true, cared as little then, as now, for religion in itself, but they were ardent patriots, and Druidic because patriots; they were indifferent what the national religion was, provided it was thoroughly anti-foreign, anti-Roman — that it was thoroughly British. Nothing, therefore, served so much to recommend Christianity and extend it in Britain, as its persecution by Rome. Common oppression drove the two religions into each other's arms, and finally united them in so indissoluble a union, that we cannot now separate in British Christianity the Druidic from the Christian element. Two events now occurred which crowned the national hatred towards both the arms and religion of Rome, and, in the same degree, disposed Druidism to identify its sufferings with those of Christianity — these were the Boadicean outrage and the Menai massacre.

Orders were issued from Rome to Suetonius Paulinus to extirpate, at any cost, the chief seat of Druidism among the Cymry, or Western Britons. Seneca, who still, in some respects, acted as Nero's adviser, demanded repayment, at the same time, of his loan to the Iceni, charging exorbitant interest. The Icenic senate demurred; whereon Caius Decius, the Roman praefect at Caistor, was instructed to take possession of all the temples, castles, and palaces belonging to the state. These orders were vigorously executed. Prasutagus, the king, dying in the midst of these measures, left Nero co-heir, with his two daughters, to his accumulated treasures. On the pretext that the whole of the royal hoard came under the denomination of public property, Decius proceeded to seize it. Resistance being made, the legionaries stormed the palace, perpetrated the most inhuman outrages on the persons of Queen Victoria and her daughters, and carried the treasures off to the Castra. Not content with these atrocities, Decius confiscated, in direct violation of the Claudian treaty, the estates of many of the Icenic *blaenorion,* or nobility. The Iceni sent Venusius to Arviragus, adjuring the Roman protectorate, and placing themselves and the Coraniaid at his disposal. Suetonius, meanwhile, by forced marches along the Wyddelian road, had reached the banks of the Menai. On either side extended the *myvyrion,* or colleges, and the cemeteries of the ancient religion, the tumuli of which are yet traceable. Here reposed, between the soaring ramparts of Snowdon, the sacred mountain, the Zion of Cymru, and the blue waters of the unexplored Atlantic, the fathers of the British Isle: chiefs whose ashes for fifteen hundred years had never been desecrated by the tramp of a foreign foe; arch-druids, the depositaries of the hoary wisdom of the East; kings whose Cimbric names had carried terror over the continents of Europe and Asia. Through these sanctuaries of so many and such ancient memories, the regulated march of the mailed legions of Rome now resounded. Anglesey was then known as Mon, and ecclesiastically, from the number of Druidic groves which covered it, sweeping down to the margin of the Menai, as Ynys Tywyll, the dark isle. The massacre of the Druidic priests and priestesses which ensued is graphically described by Tacitus. It was a complete surprise. Effecting the passage of the Menai, opposite the present seat of the Marquis of Anglesey (Plas Newydd), Seutonius gave the colleges to the flame and their inmates to the sword, the resistance attempted by the native force on the spot being easily overcome. The myvyrion were levelled with the soil, and for many nights and days the waters of the Menai were illuminated with the glare of the conflagrations of the sacred *luci* — the favourite haunts of Druidic meditation and philosophy. Tacitus endeavours to palliate this foul wholesale assassination of the ministers of religion, by stating that the Druids were in the habit of sacrificing the Roman prisoners of war on their altars. The Romans themselves, we know, after exhibiting them in triumph, slaughtered every captive king and chief in the Tarpeian dungeons, whilst the privates were condemned in thousands to butcher each other on the public altar, or the arena of the circus, in the gladiatorial games — even the vestal virgins smiling on the sanguinary holocausts. The immolation, on the other hand, of Roman prisoners by the Druids, rests on the solitary assertion of an enemy who, with a like scandalous indifference to truth, terms almost in the same page the Christian religion itself 'a destructive superstition.' [7] The news of the massacre was no sooner diffused through Britain than it excited the nation to frenzy. The war from this moment became a religious war; a crusade accompanied with all the frightful and remorseless cruelties on either side which have in all ages distinguished such hostilities. [8] The Iceni and Coranidae had entirely forfeited the name of Britons, and theoppression alone might have been regarded in the light of a just retribution, but the Menai massacre merged all other feelings in one torrent of universal indignation and horror. Boadicea soon found herself at the head of 120,000 men in arms. The Roman accounts impress us vividly with the profound gloom in which their forces were plunged, by the heavy shadows of the forthcoming disasters. Portent on portent is recorded. At Colchester the statue of Victory, like that of Dagon at Joppa, fell backward and was shattered to fragments. A Pythoness, agitated, like Cassandra on the eve of the fall of

Troy, with the insuppressible spirit of divination, caused the streets to re-echo with the cry — "Death is at hand." In the senate-house the British warcry, uttered by invisible tongues, terrified and dispersed the councillors. The theatres resounded with the shocks and groans of a field of battle. In the waters of the Thames appeared the mirage of a Roman colony subverted and in ruins. The channel between Dover and Calais ran at high tide with blood. On the tide receding, the sands revealed, in long lines, the impressions of files of bodies laid out for burial. The Menai massacre had, in fact, terrified the consciences of its perpetrators, as it had roused to fury the passions of the whole Druidic population. The return of Caràdoc also about this period to Siluria, though bound by solemn stipulation, which he faithfully observed, not to bear arms again against Rome, augmented the general commotion. The British army, assembled at Caer Llyr (Leicester) under Venusius, was harangued by Boadicea in person. Boadicea was a near relative of Claudia. We have seen the latter princess cultivating the *belles lettres,* throwing her palace open to Martial and the *literati* of the capital of Europe, receiving apostles, establishing the first Christian Church in her own household, uniting the graces of religion with refined art and high personal accomplishments. This is the royal Christian lady, such as we should expect to find, presiding, surrounded by the *élite* of Roman society, over the household of a Roman senator of ample possessions and powerful connexions. Dion Cassius gives us a sister picture of her cousin the Druidic queen, under very different circumstances during the same year in Britain. It is a grand and imposing composition, quite unique in history. Greece and Rome shew us nothing like it. The Maid of Orleans, in more modern times, is the only approach to it, but all the terrible features are supplanted by gentler ones. We see a queen, stung to madness by the wrongs which most nearly affect womanhood, leading a whole nation to battle; the sense of injury has changed her whole nature into that of a Bellona, an incarnate goddess of war, and she lives only for revenge. In her eyes every Roman is a monster already doomed. She would have been less than woman not to have felt her dishonour, more than human not to have panted for the hour of retribution. "Boadicea," writes Dion, "ascended the general's tribunal; her stature exceeded the ordinary height of woman; her appearance itself carried terror; her aspect was calm and collected, but her voice had become deep and pitiless. Her hair falling in long golden tresses as low as her hips, was collected round her forehead by a golden coronet; she wore a tartan dress fitting closely to the bosom, but below the waist expanding in loose folds as a gown; over it was a chlamys, or military cloak. In her hand she bore a spear. She addressed the Britons as follows." — We give only her peroration: —

"I thank thee! I worship thee! I appeal to thee a woman to a woman, O Andraste! I rule not, like Nitocris, over beasts of burden, as are the effeminate nations of the East, nor, like Semiramis, over tradesmen and traffickers, nor, like the man-woman Nero, over slaves and eunuchs — such is the precious knowledge these foreigners introduce amongst us — but I rule over Britons, little versed indeed in craft and diplomacy, but born and trained to the game of war: men who, in the cause of liberty, stake down their lives, the lives of their wives and children, their lands and property. Queen of such a race, I implore thine aid for freedom, for victory over enemies infamous for the wantonness of the wrongs they inflict, for their perversions of justice, for their contempt of religion, for their insatiable greed; a people that revel in unmanly pleasures, whose affections are more to be dreaded and abhorred than their enmity. Never let a foreigner bear rule over me or these my countrymen: never let slavery reign in this island. Be thou for ever, O goddess of manhood and of victory, sovereign and queen in Britain." [9]

Colchester was carried on the first assault by the British army. The temple, garrisoned by the veterans, held out for two days, then shared the same fate. Petilius Cerealis, the Roman lieutenant, was defeated, with the loss of the ninth legion, at Coggeshall (Cocci Collis). Cerealis himself, with a few horsemen, escaped into camp. The municipal town of Verulam was then stormed, gutted, and burnt. London had received a Roman garrison, under the name of a colony, within its walls. Against it the British army, now swelled to 230,000 men, directed its vengeance. A battle was fought and lost in its defence, at Ambresbury, between Waltham and Epping. [10] Such of the inhabitants as possessed the means fled, at the approach of the British Queen, to Regnum and Rutupium. The rest, including the Roman citizens and foreign merchants, took refuge with the garrison in the fortifications of the Prastorium, extending from the temple of Diana to the White Mount. The ramparts were escaladed, the city fired, public and private edifices reduced indiscriminately to ashes, the walls levelled, and above 40,000 residents put to the sword. Leaving behind this terrible example of a metropolis in conflagration, quenched with blood, Victoria swept westward to intercept Paulinus. Tacitus records but two, Dion many engagements, between her and the Roman forces. Her British epithet, Buddig, or Vuddig (the Victorians), implies that in more than one battle success followed her standard. Tacitus localizes the last battle on the margin of Epping forest — a plain error. The British traditions place it on the Wyddelian road, near the modern town of Newmarket, in Flintshire. The names still attached to the various sites of the field confirm this statement. Here are "Cop Paulinus," the "Hill of Arrows," the "Hill of Carnage," the "Hollow of Woe," the "Knoll of the Melee," the "Hollow of Execution," the "Field of the Tribunal," the "Hollow of No Quarter." Half-amile further is a monolith, the "Stone of Lamentation," and on the road to Caerwys was formerly — now removed to Downing — the "Stone of the Grave of Vuddig." Turning to the pages of Dion, we read the description of a conflict such as these names suggest — a deadly *melée* of legionaries, auxiliaries, archers, cavalry, charioteers, mingled together and swaying to and fro in all the heady currents of a long-sustained and desperate combat. Towards sunset the fortune of the day was decided in favour of the Romans. The Britons, driven back on their intrenchments, left a large number dead on the field, or prisoners in the hands of the enemy. They prepared, however, to renew the conflict, but in the interim, Victoria died, by poison according to Tacitus — in the course of nature according to the Greek historian, who adds that her obsequies were celebrated with extraordinary magnificence. Her death little affected the spirit or resources of the western and northern Britons, who continued hostilities with unabated vigour under Arviragus, Venusius, and Gwallog, or Galgacus. [11] Harassed by the same anxieties that had undermined the constitution of Ostorius Scapula, Paulinus, at the expiration of the year A.D. 61, resigned his command to Petronius Turpilianus. The whole of the Roman empire elsewhere continued to enjoy tranquility, Syria alone excepted, the disturbances in which were pacified in a few months by Corbulo. Whatever emperor occupied the throne, the military service was never deficient in generals of the highest order of ability. The war had now lasted eighteen years, and the Roman province was still limited by the Exe and Severn westward and the Humber on the north. Even within these lines its bounds fluctuated with the success of reverses or the imperial arms. [12]

[1] "Londinum vetus oppidum quod Augustam posteritas appellavit." — *Ammianus Marcellinus*, lib. xxvii. c. 8, 9. If London was not a prae-Roman city, Ammianus could not term it "an ancient city:" for supposing it founded the first year of the Claudian invasion, A.D. 43, it would still, in A.D. 350, be quite a new town; and as the Boadicean war broke out A.D. 60, it would be absurd to affirm that it rose in seventeen years to the condition described by Tacitus: "Copia negotiatorum et commeatuum maxime celebre." — *Tacit. Annal.*, lib. 1; *Hist.*, lib. L, and lib. xiv. c. 27 — 30.
[2] "Cunctator naturâ, nemo rei militaris callidior habe batur." — *Taciti Hist.*, lib. xiv. c. 20.
[3] "Magni duces, egregii exercitus." — *Tacitus, Annal.*, lib. ii. c. 24.
[4] p. 457.
[5] Richardson's Historian, p. 10.
[6] Cleland's Ancient Celtica, p. 13.
[7] Suppose we knew nothing more of the Jewish dispensation and of the Levitical priesthood than we find in Greek and Latin authors, it must be confessed we should have either to remain in total ignorance, or to embrace very absurd misconceptions. It may. however, be added, that the Greeks were equally unjust to-

wards the Romans, for no Greek writer deigns to mention the name of any of their authors, or, indeed, to suppose that they had any literature at all.

[8] In the Boadicean war, states Tacitus, no quarter was given or asked on either side: "Neque enim capere aut venumdare aliudve quod belli commercium sit," &c. — *Annal.*, lib. xiv. c. 29 — 39.

[9] Dion Cassius, *Xiphilini Excerpta,* printed in the government *Monumenta Britannica,* ad an. 58, 59.

[10] The spot of Boadicea's camp is approached across the old Ermine Street by the Camlet (Battle-way). Its figure is described in Cromwell's "Colchester," vol. 1. p. 32 as irregular, containing twelve acres, surrounded by moats and high ramparts, overgrown with oaks and hornbeams.

[11] We have elsewhere observed that the gallant and successful resistance of Britain to the Roman invasions was mainly due to the patriotic spirit and exalted doctrines with regard to the indestructibility of the soul breathed by their Druidic religion. Seneca was the indirect cause of the Boadicean war. His nephew Lucan, in the first book of *Pharsalia,* attributes the British fearlessness of death to Druidic teaching in the following fine lines: —

"Certe populi quos despicit Arctus.
Felices errore suo, quos ille timorum
Maximus haud urget, lethi metus. Inde ruendi
In ferrum mens prona vivis animaeque capaces
Mortis et ignavum rediturae parcere vitae."

Cicero had noted the fact before — "In prcelio morituri exultant Cimbri." — *Tuscul. Disp.*, lib. ii.

[12] "Non poterant Britanni sub Romana ditioni teneri," is the frank admission of the *Augustini Scriptores,* p. 68.

Chapter Four – The Tracings of the Ancient Royal Church of Britain to its Apostolic Foundations

TWO cardinal reasons, we have seen, each of national weight and extent, inclined the British mind to accept Christianity — the first, its identity in many important points with Druidism; the second, its uncompromising antagonism to the whole system of the Roman state mythology. The Roman persecution of both religions identified them still further in the popular mind. Nowhere, then, in Asia, Africa, or Europe, could the apostles find richer or a better-prepared soil for the Gospel. If we add that Britain was the only country in these ages where the Christian could profess and practise his religion free from persecution, we reasonably and antecedently conclude that a strong Christian current must have set in from both Jerusalem and Rome to this island from the first or Pentescostal days of the Church.

We shall better estimate the force of the following testimonies if we keep steadily in mind the fact that the great British Church which Augustine found A.D. 596 established in Britain and Ireland, was essentially Eastern, proclaiming by every usage in which she differed from Rome her direct and independent birth from Jerusalem and the apostles themselves in the first throes of Christianity. It is, indeed, an absurdity to go about explaining the existence of such a Church, abounding in all the characteristics of an ancient institution, deeply fixed in the native mind and soil, in any other way than by a frank acceptance of its apostolic origin. Every other attempt at solution fails us. How came these archbishoprics, bishoprics, dioceses, Christian colleges, parochial churches and endowments, royal Christian houses, genealogies of saints, immense and opulent monasteries, a whole nation of believers, to be in Britain? How came they, on their first meeting with the missionary of the Bishop of Rome, to proclaim with one voice, "We have nothing to do with Rome; we know nothing of the Bishop of Rome in his new character of the Pope; we are the British Church, the Archbishop of which is accountable to God alone, having no superior on earth." [1] This is one of those tremendous facts which rise before us like a huge mountain in the plain of history. Rome found here a Church older than herself, ramifications of which struck into the very heart of the Continent, the missionary triumphs of which in Italy itself in the life of Augustine were greater than his own among the British Saxons; for Columba and his associates from the primitive colleges in Ireland were the evangelizers of the barbarian conquerors, the Lombards, of Northern Italy. The Gallican Church was entirely one with the British in this opposition to Roman assumptions. The archbishops of Treves were, as we learn from the Tungrensian Chronicles, always supplied from Britain. Treves and Rheims became the headquarters of Gallic liberties, and here rose, under Hincmar, as powerful a resistance as in Britain to Italian supremacy. The Briton could never understand why, because Rome professed certain truths, she should arrogate spiritual despotism over all who held the same. He does not appear to have troubled himself about her errors and corruptions; these he regarded as her own matters, with which, as not belonging to him, he did not interfere. Cadvan, Prince of Wales, expresses himself thus to the Abbot of Bangor: — "All men may hold the same truths, yet no man thereby be drawn into slavery to another. If the Cymry believed all that Rome believes, that would be as strong reason for Rome obeying us as for us to obey Rome. It suffices for us that we obey the truth. If other men obey the truth, are they, therefore, to become subject to us? Then were the truth of Christ made slavery unto men, and not freedom."

The soldier who interrogated Augustine at the oak of Conference seems, in like manner, to treat the question between them as one quite apart from doctrine.

"Does Rome possess all the truth?"

"All."

"And you say we do — our usages only differ. Now of two men, if both have all their limbs and senses complete, both are equal. Because the Romans have noses and we have noses, must we either cut off our noses to be Romans? must all who have noses be subject to the Romans? Why, then, should all who hold the faith be subject to Rome because she holds the faith?"

This rough, broad reasoning allowed almost identity in doctrine and practices to be maintained by any Christian with Rome, or any other Church, without in the most remote degree admitting any claim Rome might advance on the ground of such identity. The Briton thus had his festivals, processions, floral decorations, antiphonal choirs, cathedrals — an immense deal in common with Rome — but he had had them for centuries before Papal Rome was ever heard of. And he would have ridiculed the notion that he was to give up a good thing because Rome also had it, as he scorned the idea that a community in such things constituted the shadow of a title on the part of Rome to his allegiance. His position, in fact, was a very strong one, — thoroughly Catholic, thoroughly anti-fanatical, and at the same time thoroughly anti-papal: and he knew its strength, resting on historical monuments which could neither be ignored nor destroyed: around him rose hoary cathedrals, churches, abbeys, colleges, "imperishable stones of witness" that his Church was the primitive apostolical Church of Britain, — that the Papacy, with all its claims, was a novelty, an intrusion, an invention, a fable; that there never was a time when the eyes of the Christian pilgrim did not rest in this island on vast evidences bespeaking a Church subject to no other Church on earth, built on its own apostolic foundations, and recognising the apostolic Scriptures alone for its rule of faith. [2]

The general conclusion arrived at by the writers who have previously investigated this final part of our question may be given in the words of Capellus: "I scarcely know of one author, from the times of the Fathers downwards, who does not maintain that St. Paul, after his liberation, preached in every country in Western Europe, Britain included." [3] "Of St. Paul's journey to Britain," writes Bishop Burgess, "we have as satisfactory proof as any historical question can demand." [4] The same view is substantially maintained by Baronius, the Centuriators of Magdeburg, Alford or Griffith, next to Baronius the most erudite of the Roman Catholic historians; Archbishops Parker and Usher, Stillingfleet, Camden, Gibson, Cave, Nelson, Allix, &c.

Let us preface the *catena authoritatum* on this point with a few general testimonies from widely different quarters.

"The cradle of the ancient British Church was a royal one, herein being distinguished from all other Churches: for it proceeded from the daughter of the British king, Caractacus, Claudia Rufina, a royal virgin, the same who was afterwards the wife of Aulus Rufus Pudens, the Roman senator, and the mother of a family of saints and martyrs." [5]

"We have abundant evidence that this Britain of ours received the Faith, and that from the disciples of Christ Himself, soon after the crucifixion of Christ." [6]

"Britain in the reign of Constantine had become the seat of a flourishing and extensive Church." [7]

"Our forefathers, you will bear in mind, were not generally converted, as many would fain represent, by Roman missionaries. The heralds of salvation who planted Christianity in most parts of England were trained in British schools of theology, and were firmly attached to those national usages which had descended to them from the most venerable antiquity." [8]

"The Christian religion began in Britain within fifty years of Christ's ascension." [9]

"Britain, partly through Joseph of Arimathaea, partly through Fugatus and Damianus, was of all kingdoms the first that received the Gospel." [10]

"We can have no doubt that Christianity had taken root and flourished in Britain in the middle of the second century." [11]

"It is perfectly certain, that before St. Paul had come to Rome Aristobulus was absent in Britain, and it is confessed by all that Claudia was a British lady." [12]

"The faith which was adopted by the nation of the Britons in the year of our Lord 165, was preserved inviolate, and in the enjoyment of peace, to the time of the Emperor Diocletian." [13]

Let us now trace our way back from the time of Venerable Bede, A.D. 740, step by step, to the apostolic era and the apostles themselves.

In the seventh century we have a galaxy of Christian bishops in England, Wales, Ireland and Scotland, whose names alone would make a considerable catalogue.

In the year A.D. 596 we have the Augustine mission landing in Kent, followed by three conferences with the bishops of the British Church. In A.D. 600, Venantius Fortunatus, in his Christian Hymns, speaks of Britain as having been evangelized by St. Paul. [14]

In A.D. 542, Gildas writes: "We certainly know that Christ, the True Sun, afforded His light, the knowledge of His precepts, to our island in the last year of the reign of Tiberius Caesar." [15]

In A.D. 500-540, we have various productions of Christian bards, such as Taliesin and Aneurin, emanating from the courts of the Christian sovereigns of Britain — one of the latter, "The Crowned Babe" (i.e., Christ), interesting as the earliest European specimen, of any length, of rhyme in poetry: it is composed in the ancient British tongue.

In the year A.D. 408 Augustine of Hippo asks, "How many churches are there not erected in the British isles which lie in the ocean?" [16] And about the same time Arnobius writes: "So swiftly runs the word of God that though in several thousand years God was not known, except among the Jews, now, within the space of a few years, His word is concealed neither from the Indians in the East nor from the Britons in the West." [17]

Theodoretus in A.D. 435 testifies: "Paul, liberated from his first captivity at Rome, preached the Gospel to the Britons and others in the West. Our fishermen and publicans not only persuaded the Romans and their tributaries to acknowledge the Crucified and His laws, but the Britons also and the Cimbri (Cymry)." [18]

To the same purport in his commentary on 2 Timothy iv. 16: "When Paul was sent by Festus on his appeal to Rome, he travelled, after being acquitted, into Spain, and thence extended his excursions into other countries, and to the islands surrounded by the sea."

More express testimony to Paul's preaching in Britain could not be delivered, nor from a more unexceptional quarter. Theodoret was Bishop of Cyropolis, attended both the General Councils of Ephesus (A.D. 431), against the Nestorians, and of Chalcedon, A.D. 451, consisting of 600 bishops. As an excellent interpreter of Scripture, and a writer of ecclesiastical history, he deservedly ranks high.

Chrysostom, Patriarch of Constantinople, supplies (A.D. 402) cumulative evidence of the existence of pure British Christianity. "The British Isles," he writes, "which are beyond the sea, and which lie in the ocean, have received the virtue of the Word. Churches are there founded and altars erected. Though thou shouldst go to the ocean, to the British Isles, there thou shouldst hear all men everywhere discoursing matters out of the Scriptures, with another voice, indeed, but not another faith, with a different tongue but the same judgment." [19]

"From India to Britain," writes St. Jerome (A.D. 378), "all nations resound with the death and resurrection of Christ." [20]

In A.D. 320, Eusebius, Bishop of Caesarea, speaks of apostolic missions to Britain as a matter of notoriety: "The apostles passed beyond the ocean to the isles called the Brittanic Isles." [21]

The first part of the fourth century is the era of Constantine the Great and his mother Helena. Gibbon, with that perversity which beset him as a mania in dealing with the leading facts of Christianity, strives to persuade himself that Constantine and Helen were not Britons, but natives of some obscure village in the East; [22] his sole support for such a supposition being the fragment of an anonymous author, appended to Ammianus Marcellinus. "The man must be mad," states Baronius, "who, in the face of universal antiquity, refuses to believe that Constantine and his mother were Britons, born in Britain." [23] Archbishop Usher delivers a catalogue of twenty continental authorities in the affirmative — not one to the contrary. The Panegyrics of the Emperors, the genealogy of his own family, as recited by one of his descendants, Constantine Palaeologus, native records and traditions, ail the circumstances of his career, demonstrate Constantine a Briton, bred in the strongest British ideas. "It is well known," states Sozomen, "the great Constantine received his Christian education in Britain." [24] "Helen was unquestionably a British princess," writes Melancthon. [25] "Christ," declares Pope Urban in his Brief, Britannia, "shewed to Constantine the Briton the victory of the cross for his sceptre." "Constantine," writes Polydore Vergil, "born in Britain, of a British mother, proclaimed Emperor in Britain beyond doubt, made his natal soil a participator in his glory." [26] Constantine was all this and more — by his mother's side he was the heir and representative of the royal Christian dynasty of Britain, as a glance at the table on the next page will serve to show.

The policy of Constantine, in carrying out which for twenty years with admirable wisdom and inflexible purpose he was supported by armies levied for the most part in his native British dominions, consisted in extending to the whole Roman world the system of constitutional Christianity which had long been established in Britain. But his religious sympathies, as well as those of his mother, were wholly Eastern, not Roman. They were those of the British Church. They revolved round Jerusalem, and the Holy Land, and not Rome. Constantine made but two brief visits, during his long reign, to the Italian capital. Helen spent all her declining years in restoring the churches and sacred sites of Palestine. The objects of Constantine's life are well explained by him in one of his edicts: "We call God to witness, the Saviour of all men, that in assuming the government, we are influenced solely by these two considerations — the uniting of the empire in one faith, and the restoration of peace to a world rent to pieces by the insanity of religious persecution." Regarded in his threefold character of general, statesman, and legislator, the British founder of secular Christendom may justly be considered the greatest of the Roman emperors. The British Church was represented during his reign by native bishops at the Councils of Aries, A.D. 308, and Nice, A.D. 325. [27]

In A.D. 300 the Diocletian persecution raged in Britain, but was stopped in one year by Constantius Chlorus, continuing to ravage the rest of the empire for eighteen years. We have elsewhere given a list of the British martyrs who perished in it. We cannot doubt that we stand, during these

Royal Christian Dynasty of Ancient Britain

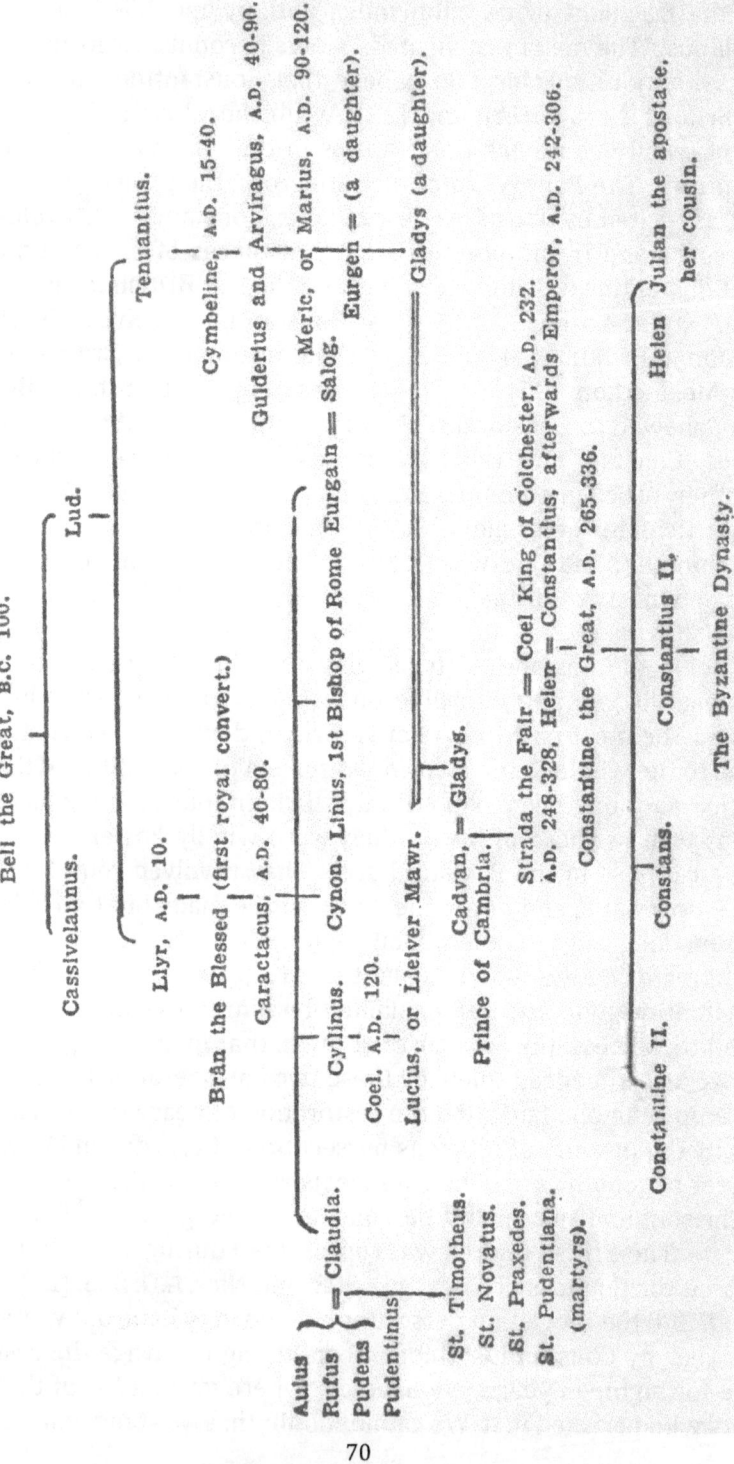

centuries, in the midst of a Church as broad and thoroughly national as the present Protestant establishment; indeed, in one chief respect more so, for the present national Church of England is not that of the people of Scotland, Wales, or Ireland, whereas the ancient British Church embraced all these populations in its fold. Their very names indicate the broader national character of the ancient and primitive Church, one being the British Church, or Church of Britain, the other the Church of England.

Continuing to trace the British Church back, we find Origen, A.D. 230, alluding thus to its existence: "The divine goodness of our Lord and Saviour is equally diffused among the Britons, the Africans, and other nations of the world." [28]

In A.D. 230, however, Britain had been re-incorporated in the Roman empire. What was the case in A.D. 192-198, in the reign of Commodus, when it proclaimed its independence, and the British legions elected Albinus Caesar? Was the Church confined to the Roman province then insurgent, or were the stubborn British tribes — the Cymri, the Caledonii, the Picts, whom no efforts of peace or war could succeed in bringing to acknowledge the right of a foreigner to plant hostile foot in Britain — within its pale? Tertullian, who flourished during the war of Commodus in Britain, which Dion Cassius terms "the most dangerous in which the empire during his time had been engaged," says expressly that the regions in Britain which the Roman arms had failed to penetrate professed Christianity for their religion. "The extremities of Spain, the various parts of Gaul, the regions of Britain which have never been penetrated by the Roman arms, have received the religion of Christ." [29] We have seen that the British Church had, long before Tertullian's age, founded the Churches of Gaul, Lorraine, and Switzerland, and that its missionaries had made their way into Pannonia. Coming nearer Rome itself, we find that in Tertullian's own age a missionary of the British Church founded, A.D. 170, the Church of Tarentum. This was St. Cadval, after whom the cathedral at Tarento is still named. [30] Not only, therefore, did the British Church, A.D. 170, embrace Roman and Independent Britain, but it had struck its roots in France, Switzerland, Germany, and the extremities of Italy.

We now come to A.D. 120-150, within the era of the disciples of the apostles. It is certain from St. Paul's own letters to the Romans and to Timothy, that he was on the most intimate and affectionate terms with the mother of Rufus Pudens, with Pudens himself, with Claudia his wife, and Linus. The children of Claudia and Pudens were instructed in the faith by St. Paul himself. The eldest was baptized Timotheus, after Timothy, Bishop of Ephesus, the Apostle's "beloved son in Christ." The four, Timotheus, Novatus, Praxedes, Pudentiana, with their father, Pudens, sealed at different times their faith with their blood in Rome, and were, with Linus, the first Britons who were added to the glorious army of martyrs. And, Pudens excepted, they were not only martyrs, but royal martyrs; not only royal martyrs, but martyrs of the most patriotic and heroic blood in Britain. Let us confirm these statements by the evidences of primitive antiquity.

The reader will recollect the "natal day" of a martyr is the day of his martyrdom.

Pudens suffered A.D. 96, Linus A.D. 90; Pudentiana suffered on the anniversary of her father's martyrdom, in the third persecution, A.D. 107; Novatus in the fifth persecution, A.D. 139, when his brother Timotheus was absent in Britain, baptizing his nephew, King Lucius. [31] Shortly after his return from Britain, and in extreme old age, about his ninetieth year, Timotheus suffered with his fellow-soldier Marcus in the same city of Rome, "drunk with the blood of the martyrs of Jesus." Praxedes, the surviving sister, received her crown within the same year. Claudia alone died a natural death, in Samnium, before any of her children, A.D. 97, surviving Pudens one year. They were all interred by the side of St. Paul in the Via Ostiensis.

May 17. Natal day of the blessed Pudens, father of Praxedes and Pudentiana. He was clothed with baptism by the apostles, and watched and kept his robe pure and without wrinkle to the crown of a blameless life. [32]

November 26. Natal day of St. Linus, Bishop of Rome. [33]

May 17. Natal day of St. Pudentiana, the virgin, of the most illustrious descent, daughter of Pudens, and disciple of the holy apostle St. Paul. [34]

June 20. Natal day of St. Novatus, son of the blessed Pudens, brother of St. Timotheus the elder, and the virgins of Christ Pudentiana and Praxedes. All these were instructed in the faith by the apostles.

August 22. Natal day of St. Timotheus, son of St. Pudens, in the Via Ostiensis. [35]

September 21. Natal day of St. Praxedes, virgin of Christ, in Rome. [36]

Have we, again, any direct contemporary evidence that Linus, the first bishop of Rome, was the son of Caractacus, and brother of Claudia Britannica? Putting aside, for a moment, British genealogies and tradition, does any contemporary of St. Paul and Linus, in Rome itself, assert the fact? Undoubtedly. Clemens Romanus, who is mentioned by St. Paul, states in his epistle, the genuineness of which has never been questioned, that Linus was the brother of Claudia — "Sanctissimus Linus, frater Claudiae." [37] Clemens succeeded Cletus within twelve years of the death of Linus, as third bishop of Rome. He had also been associated with the British missionary Mansuetus, in evangelizing Illyria. His sources of information are, therefore, unquestionable. St. Paul lived, according to all evidence, whenever he was at Rome, whether in custody at large (*libera custodiá*) or free, in the bosom of the Oaudian family. There is no dispute that Claudia herself was purely British, and whether Linus was her son or brother, the British character of the family, and the close, the domestic ties of affection between such family and St. Paul, are equally manifest. The relationship is, in many important regards, more intimate between St. Paul and the British mind — that mind being the leading, because the royal, influence in Britain — in the domestic circle and family worship of the Claudian palace at Rome, than when he addressed the British people themselves in Britain.

But Clemens Romanus not only proves to us that the family which the Apostle thus honoured with his constant residence and instruction was British, that the first bishop appointed by him over the Church at Rome was of this British family, but that St. Paul himself preached in Britain, for no other interpretation can be assigned to his words, ἐπί τό τέρμα τῆς Δυοέως — "the extremity of the West." "Paul, after he had been to the extremity of the West, underwent his martyrdom before the rulers of mankind; and thus delivered from this world, went to his holy place." [38]

It may be suggested that Linus, the first bishop of Rome, was, however, some other than the brother of Claudia, mentioned by St. Paul. Not so; for if the above authorities permitted a doubt to remain, the evidence of Irenaeus as to their identity is conclusive. "The apostles," writes Irenaeus, A.D. 180, "having founded and built up the Church at Rome, committed the ministry of its supervision to Linus. This is the Linus mentioned by Paul in his Epistle to Timothy." [39]

We are not aware we should be stating anything improbable if we regarded St. Paul's domiciliation at the house of Pudens, or his being ministered to immediately before his martyrdom by Pudens, Claudia, and Linus, as additional presumptive evidence of his sojourn in Britain. At any rate, we observe that all the sympathies with which he was surrounded, after his arrival at Rome, in the Claudian family, all the influences of that family in their native country, would lead him to Britain in preference to any other land of the West. This was the great isle of the Gentiles, the centre and source of their religion, and, through his royal converts, a "mighty door and an effectual" for its conversion was opened to him.

Caractacus meanwhile continued to reside at Aber Gweryd, now St. Donat's Major (Llan Ddunwyd), in Glamorganshire, where he had built a palace, more Romano. Everything invited Paul to Britain, to follow the bishop he had already commissioned for the work of the Gospel therein, and to be the guest of the royal parent of Claudia. Considering the combination of circumstances which now favoured the execution of his long-cherished design of visiting the West of Europe, we should regard it much more extraordinary if the Apostle had not come to Britain than we do his coming here. When to this circumstantial evidence we add the written testimonies we have adduced of Eusebius, Theodoret, Clemens, and others, that he positively did preach in Britain, we see fair reason for concurring in Bishop Burgess's conclusion, though the bishop had but a part of the evidence we have collected before him, "That we possess as substantial evidence, as any historical fact can require, of St. Paul's journey to Britain." [40]

There are six years of St. Paul's life to be accounted for, between his liberation from his first imprisonment and his martyrdom at Aquae Salvias in the Ostian Road, near Rome. Part certainly, the greater part perhaps, of this period, was spent in Britain — in Siluria or Cambria, beyond the bounds of the Roman empire; and hence the silence of the Greek and Latin writers upon it.

Has any portion of his doctrine or teaching in Britain come down to us? Any such would be sure to be transmitted in a British form, and most probably in that triadic form in which the Druids, the religious teachers of Britain, delivered their teaching. Now we find in the ancient British language certain triads which have never been known otherwise than as "the triads of Paul the Apostle." They are not found totidem verbis, either whole or fragmentally, in his epistles, but the morality inculcated is, of course, quite in unison with the rest of his Gospel preaching.

[1] The continental Churches admitted, for the most part, a Primacy when they rejected the Supremacy of the Bishop of Rome. The British Church admitted neither; it knew nothing of the Bishop of Rome, except on an equality with any of its own British bishops, or any other bishop in the Christian Church. The further we go back into British history, the clearer shines forth in all our laws the entire independence of the British crowns, Church, and people, of all foreign authority. All our great legal authorities concur on this point. "The ancient British Church," writes Blackstone, vol. iv. p. 105, "by whomsoever planted, was a stranger to the Bishop of Rome and all his pretended authorities." "The Britons told Augustine," writes Bacon, *Government of England,* "they would not be subject to him, nor let him pervert the ancient laws of their Church. This was their resolution, and they were as good as their word, for they maintained the liberty of their Church five hundred years after his time, and were the last of all the Churches of Europe that gave up their power to the Roman Beast, and in the person of Henry VIII, that came of their blood by Owen Tudor, the first that took that power away again."

[2] Bede's testimony as to the pure scriptural character of the teaching of the British Church is full and explicit, and he contrasts, with feelings of shame and reluctance, the apostolic lives of the British missionaries with those of his own Papal Church. Of Columba he writes. "He taught only what was contained in the prophetic, evangelic, and apostolic writings, all works of piety and charity being at the same time diligently observed." — Lib. iii. c. 41. Of Aidan: "All who resorted to him applied themselves either to reading the Scriptures or to learning Psalms." — Lib. iii. c. 5. Of Adamnan: "He was most admirably versed in the knowledge of the Scriptures." — Lib. iii. c. 15. How entirely the British Church rejected human authority in matters of faith may be collected from the saying of Columba, "Except what has been declared by the Law, the prophets, the evange-

lists, and apostles, a profound silence ought to be observed by all others on the subject of the Trinity." — Lib. iii. c. 4.

[3] Hist, of the Apostles.
[4] Independence of the British Church.
[5] Moncaeus Atrebas, the learned Gallican divine, In *Syntagma*, p. 38.
[6] Sir Henry Spelman's *Concilia*, fol., p. 1.
[7] Soames' Anglo-Saxon Church, Introd.. p. 29.
[8] Soames' Bampton Lectures, pp. 112 — 257. This statement is so true, that sixty-three years after the landing of Augustine, that is, A.D. 660, when all the Heptarchy, except Sussex, had been converted, Wini, Bishop of Winchester, was the only bishop of the Romish communion in Britain, and he had purchased his first bishopric of London from Wulfhere, King of Mercia: all the rest were British. And the cause is patent: Maelwyn or Patrick, the apostle of Ireland Ninian, the apostle of the southern Picts, Aidan of the Northumbrians, Paul Hen his successor, Columba of the Scots, Finan of the East Angles, Cad or Chad of the Mercians, were all native Britons, educated in the native colleges. The Romish succession had died down to one prelate, and Saxon Christianity was kept alive or refounded by British Christians. The succession of Augustine in Canterbury and Rochester expired in Damianus, A.D. 666.
[9] Robert Parsons the Jesuit's Three Conversions of England, vol. i. p. 26.
[10] Polydore Vergil, lib. ii.
[11] Cardwell's (Camden Prof.) Ancient History, p. 18, 1837.
[12] Alford's *Regia Fides,* vol. i. p. 19.
[13] Bede, lib. i. c. 4.
[14] "Transit et oceanum vel qua facit insula portum.
    Quasque Britannus habet terras atque ultima Thule."
[15] *De Excidio Britanniae,* p. 25.
[16] Opera, fol., Paris Edit., p. 676.
[17] Arnobius, *Ad. Psalm* cxlvii.
[18] Theodoret, *De Civ. Graze. Off.,* lib ix. Nicephorus seems to have followed Theodoretus (Niceph., lib. ii. c. 40); and Eusebius Pamphilus, lib. iv. — "ἐπί τάς καλσυμενας
[19] Chrysostomi, Orat. Ὁ Θεός Χριστός
[20] Jerome, *In Isaiam,* c. liv.; also, *Epistol.,* xiii. *ad Paulinum.*
[21] Eusebius *De Demonstratione Evangelii,* lib. iii.
[22] Naissus. Colchester, the birth-place of Helen of the Cross, has, from time immemorial, borne the cross with three crowns for its arms.
[23] Baronius, *ad ann.* 306: "Non nisi extremae dementiae hominis." Until the reign of Constantine the Roman Christians had no other church than the Titulus to worship in: "Ante Constantini imperium templa Romae non habuerint Christiani," observes Bale (Scriptores Britan., p. 17.) The Pope, it is well known, claims the sovereignty of the States of the Church by right of the decree of the British Emperor Constantine making them over in free gift to the Bishop of Rome. That this decree was a forgery no one doubts; it was, however, confirmed by Pepin. By the papal Church's own showing, it is infinitely more indebted to the ancient British Church and sovereigns than they ever were to it. Without the benefactions of the Claudian family and Constantine, it would never have risen above the

character given it by Pius the First, the brother of Hermas Pastor — "Pauper Senatus Christi." For its earthly aggrandisement it is mainly indebted to ancient British liberality.

[24] Sozomen, *Eccles. Hist.*, lib. i. c. v. So Eumenius, in his Panegyric on Constantius to Constantine: "He begot thee in the very flower of his age." — *Pan.* 9.
[25] *Epistola*, p. 189.
[26] *Historic Brit.*, p. 381.
[27] The archbishopric of York was founded, at the request of Helen, by Constantius the Emperor, A.D. 290. Its second archbishop, Socrates, was martyred in the Diocletian persecution.
[28] Origen, *In Psalm* cxlix.
[29] Tertullian, Def. Fidei, p. 179.
[30] MS. Vellum of the Church of Tarentum; Catalogue of Saints in the Vatican, published A.D. 1641; Moronus, De Ecclesia Tarentina.
[31] All authors concur in this fact, though all do not see how naturally it followed that the relationship between the royal house of Britain and its branch settled in Rome.
[32] Martyr. Romana, ad diem Maii 17. To the same effect the Martyrologies of Ado, Usuard and Esquilinus.
[33] Martyr, Rom., ad diem; Martyrologies of Ado; Greek Menologies; Usuard, &c.
[34] Martyr. Rom., ad diem; Ado, &c.
[35] Martyr. Rom., Ado, Asuard, Greek Menol.
[36] Martyr. Rom., Ado, &c.
[37] In the Oxford edition of Junius, published A.D. 1633, "The son of Claudia." *Apostol ci Patres*, lib. vii. c. 47; *Apostolici Constitutiones*, c. 46. The Apostolic Constitutions may or may not be what their present title infers; but no scholar who peruses the opinions *pro et contra*, collected by Iltigius, (*De Patribus Apostolicis*), Buddaeus, (*Isagoge in Theologiam*), and Baratier, (*De Successione Vrimorum Episcoporum*), will assign them a later date than A.D. 150. The mention of Linus in them runs thus: "Concerning those bishops who have been ordained in our lifetime, we make known to you that they are these: Of Antioch, Euodius ordained by me, Peter; of the Church of Rome, Linus, the (son) of Claudia, was first ordained by Paul, and after Linus' death, Clemens the second, ordained by me, Peter." Lib. i. c. 46. In the original, Δίνος μέυ ὁ κλαυδίας π ρῶτος ὑπό Πούγου Analogy requires υἱός to be supplied, but the relationship might have been so well known as to render αὁελφς superfluous.
[38] Clement. Rom., Epistola ad Corinthios, c. 5. The passage *in extenso* runs thus: "To leave the examples of antiquity, and to come to the most recent, let us take the noble examples of our own times. Let us place before our eyes the good apostles. Peter, through unjust odium, underwent not one or two, but many sufferings; and having undergone his martyrdom, he went to the place of glory to which he was entitled. Paul, also, having seven times worn chains, and been hunted and stoned, received the prize of such endurance. For he was the herald of the Gospel in the West as well as in the East, and enjoyed the illustrious reputation of the faith in teaching the whole world to be righteous. And after he had been to the extremity of the West, he suffered martyrdom before the sovereigns

of mankind; and thus delivered from this world, he went to his holy place, the most brilliant example of stedfastness that we possess."

[39] Irenaei Opera, lib. iii. c. 1. Irenaeus was born in Asia, became a disciple of Polycarp Bishop ol Smyrna, afterwards a presbyter of Lyons, whence he was sent as a delegate to the Asiatic Churches. He succeeded Photinus in the bishopric, and suffered under Severus.

[40] The ancient MS. in Merton College, Oxord, which purports to contain a series of letters between St. Paul and Seneca, has more than one allusion to St. Paul's residence in Siluria.

Had the large collection of British archives and MSS. deposited at Verulam as late as A.D. 860, descended to our times, invaluable light would have been thrown on this as on many other subjects of native interest. Amongst these works were the Poems and Hymns of Claudia. Vide Matthew of Westminster, William of Malmesbury, "Life of Eadmer."

Triads of Paul the Apostle

"There are three sorts of men: The man of God, who renders good for evil; the man of men, who renders good for good and evil for evil; and the man of the devil, who renders evil for good.

"Three kinds of men are the delights of God: the meek; the lovers of peace; the lovers of mercy.

"There are three marks of the children of God: Gentle deportment; a pure conscience; patient suffering of injuries.

"There are three chief duties demanded by God: Justice to every man; love; humility.

"In three places will be found the most of God: Where He is mostly sought; where He is mostly loved; where there is least of self.

"There are three things following faith in God: A conscience at peace; union with heaven; what is necessary for life.

"Three ways a Christian punishes an enemy: By forgiving him; by not divulging his wickedness; by doing him all the good in his power.

"The three chief considerations of a Christian: Lest he should displease God; lest he should be a stumblingblock to man; lest his love to all that is good should wax cold.

"The three luxuries of a Christian feast: What God has prepared; what can be obtained with justice to all; what love to all may venture to use.

"Three persons have the claims and privileges of brothers and sisters: the widow; the orphan; the stranger." [1]

The evangelical simplicity of these precepts, contrasting so forcibly with monkish and mediaeval inventions and superstitions, favours the traditional acceptance of their Pauline origin. Their preservation is due to the Cor of Hid.

The foundation of the great abbey of Bangor Iscoed is assigned by tradition to St. Paul. Its discipline and doctrine were certainly known as "the Rule of Paul" (*Pauli Regula* , and over each of the four gates was engraved his precept, "If a man will not work, neither let him eat." Its abbots regarded themselves as his successors; they were always men of the highest grade in society, and generally of the blood royal. Bede and other authors state the number of monks in it at 2,100. The scholars amounted to many thousands. Pelagius was its twentieth abbot. St. Hilary and St. Benedict term it "Mater omnium monasteriorum," the mother of all monasteries. The first Egyptian monastery was founded by Pachomius, A.D. 360. [2]

In what language did St. Paul preach in Britain? This question, if pursued, would open an interesting but difficult investigation. Every apostle, by the Pentecostal inspiration, possessed the command of every known tongue then in the world. This supernatural faculty was part of the "power from on high" with which they were endowed, and the lingual credential of their divine mission. Of the fact that Paul preached in the British tongue we have no evidence; neither have we any that he ever preached in Latin; yet with both languages he must, as an apostle, have been familiar. We infer he often preached in both. The Druids in their sacred writings used the Bardic alphabet, of forty-two characters; but in their civil transactions, as Caesar informs us, the Greek alphabet. St. Paul wrote all his Epistles in Greek, and Greek continued some time after the apostolic age the language of the Church at Rome. The royal family of Britain were, as we have seen, ardently attached to both Greek and Latin literature. Cymbeline and Llyr, the old generation, had received their education, which must necessarily have been the highest Rome could impart, from Augustus Caesar himself. Caractacus must, unless we have recourse to the rather violent supposition that Claudius, who heard, and Tacitus, who has recorded, his oration, were proficients in British, have delivered himself in Latin. [3] Paul, it is certain, used the tongue of the people in preaching to the people. The canon he laid down for the Corinthian Church was that which he practised himself: "If I know not the meaning of the voice, I shall be to him that speaketh a barbarian, and he that speaketh shall be to me a barbarian...I would rather in the church speak five words with my understanding than ten thousand words in an unknown tongue." [4] He must, therefore, according to this rule, have preached to the Britons in their vernacular tongue.

By the conversion of the British dynasty in its various members, a very important class of prophecies were fulfilled. The expressions, also, "the ends of the earth," "the uttermost parts of the earth," "the isles afar off," used by Isaiah, are precisely those which the Roman authors also used to designate Britain.

From the captivity of Caractacus and the life of St. Paul in the family of his daughter Claudia at Rome, to the turning of the Roman empire into Christendom, the history of the royal dynasty of Britain in connection with the Church of Christ is indeed one long, continuous, and exact verification of Scriptural prophecy. [5]

Against the British Church itself no charge of heretical doctrine has at any time been advanced, though the heresiarch, the very prince of heretics — Pelagius, was nursed in her bosom. Bede's reluctant testimony is, on this point, decisive. Whilst the Christian Churches in Asia, Africa, and on the Continent of Europe were overrun with false doctrines, the British Church grew up and covered with its shade the whole nation, untroubled for the space of four centuries by any root of bitterness. It is reasonable to infer that the foundations of such a Church were very deeply and faithfully laid by the hands of wise master-builders. According to the foundation rose the superstructure, resting on these four pillars — St. Paul, Simon Zelotes, Joseph, Aristobulus. Its great evangelist in the second century, St. Timotheus, the baptizer of his nephew King Lucius and of his nobility at Winchester, had also received the faith from the mouth of Paul himself. This unanimity of faith in the founders impressed itself on the Church they founded, which "continued in the things it had learned and been assured of, knowing from whom it had learned them."

Having thus first surveyed the religions of the ancient world at the birth of Christianity, and next traced the introduction of the latter, and its progress in Britain, a bird's-eye view will shew us the following Churches, making up the Catholic Church sixty-six years after the Incarnation: — In Palestine — Jerusalem, Samaria, Caesarea, Lydda; in Assyria — Babylon; in Syria — Antioch, Damascus; in Asia-Minor — Antioch of Pisidia, Iconium, Lystra, Ephesus, Smyrna, Sardis, Thyatira, Pergamos, Philadelphia, Caesarea in Cappadocia; Laodicea, Colosse, Galatia; in Greece — Athens, Corinth, Thessalonica, Beraea, Philippi, Crete; in Egypt — Alexandria; in Italy — Rome; in Gaui — Lyons; in Britain — Cor Avàlon (Glastonbury), Cor Salog (Old Sarum), Cor Hid (Llan Hid) in Siluria.

The force of the testimony for St. Paul's residence in Britain may be more clearly estimated by comparing it with that for St. Peter's at Rome. The earliest testimony in favour of the latter is that of Irenaeus, bishop of Lyons, A.D. 180, [6] prior to which we find no indication in the Scriptures or ecclesiastical authors that St. Peter ever visited or ever intended to visit Rome, which, as a Gentile Church over which St. Paul in the most pointed manner claimed jurisdiction, [7] was certainly not within the province of the apostle of the circumcision. Britain, on the contrary, was within Paul's province, placed already, as Ephesus and Crete had been, by Paul himself under one of his bishops, Aristobulus. If we are to concede that St. Peter founded the Roman Church in person, much more are we compelled by infinitely stronger evidence to acknowledge that St. Paul in person founded the British Church. [8]

Of St. Paul's life after quitting Britain no particulars have descended to us. After visiting Asia we find him in the last scene of his life returned to the bosom of the British royal family at Rome. In his farewell charges to Timothy he sends him the greetings of Pudens, Linus, and Claudia. These, with that of Eubulus, the cousin of Claudia, are the only names of the brethren mentioned by him; these ministered to him on the eve of his martyrdom, these attended him when he was on the block of the state lictor at Aquae Salviae, a little out of Rome, and these consigned his remains with their own hands to the Pudentinian family tomb on the Ostian Road. Like his Divine Master, "he made his grave with the rich in his death." Linus, Claudia and Pudens and their four children, when God in His appointed time called them to receive the same crown of the Cross, were buried by his side: the other royal converts, Bran, Caractacus, Cyllinus, and Eurgain died peaceably in Britain, and were interred in the cor of Hid in Siluria. All — kings, heroes, apostles, martyrs, saints — were united in the kingdom of light, in the joy of their Lord. [9]

[1] Ancient British Triads; Triads of Paul the Apostle.
[2] "Pelagius heresiarchus ex Britanniâ oriundus famati illius collegii Bangorensis praepositus erat in quo Christianorum philosophorum 2,100 militabant suarum manuum laboribus juxta Pauli doctrinam victitantes." — *Vita Pelagii*, p. 3.
[3] Claudia herself was the authoress of a volume of epigrams, a volume of elegies, and a volume of sacred poems or hymns. Copies of these were preserved in the library at Verulam as late as the thirteen century.
[4] i Cor. xiv. ii, 19: It was the uniform practice of Christians, from the earliest times, to read the Scriptures in the vulgar tongue, and it was not till the period of Charlemagne that Latin became the language of the Church services. Vide Usher's *Historia Dogmatica*. No two causes contributed so much to the declension of Christianity and the progress of Mahometanism, as the suppression by the Church of Rome of the vernacular Scriptures, and her adoption of image-worship.
[5] A few of these prophecies we subjoin: —
"It is a light thing that thou shouldest be My servant to raise up the tribes of Jacob, and to restore the outcasts of Israel: I will also give thee for a light to the Gentiles, that thou mayest be My salvation unto the ends of the earth. Kings shall see and arise; princes also shall worship. Behold they shall come from the north and from the west. Kings shall be thy nursing-fathers and queens thy nursing-mothers. Arise, shine, for thy light is come, and the glory of the Lord is risen upon thee. The Gentiles shall come to thy light, and kings to the brightness of thy rising. Thy sons shall come from far, and thy daughters shall be nursed at thy side.

The sons of strangers shall build up thy walls, and kings shall minister unto thee. Thou shalt suck the milk of the Gentiles, and shalt suck the breast of kings. I will set My sign among them, and send them that escape of them unto the nations, unto the isles afar off, and they shall declare My glory unto the Gentiles. They shall inherit the land for ever, the branch of My planting." — Isaiah xlix, lx, lxvi.

[6] Irenaei Opera, lib. iii. c. 1: "Matthew published his Gospel among the Hebrews in his own language while Peter and Paul were engaged in evangelizing and founding the Christian Church at Rome."

[7] "My apostleship for obedience to the faith among all nations, among whom are ye also...that I might have some fruit among you also, as among other Gentiles."— Rom. i. 5, 13.

[8] If we desired to strengthen from Roman Catholic evidence the apostolical foundations of the British Church, or to insist that it can with equal justice, at least, as the Roman Church, claim St. Peter amongst its founders, it would not be difficult to adduce the affirmative evidence of Roman Catholic authorities upon the point. Cornelius a Lapide, in answering the question "How came St. Paul not to salute St. Peter in his Epistle to the Romans," states, "Peter, banished with the rest of the Jews from Rome by the edict of Claudius, was absent in Britain." (*Cornelius à Lapide, in Argumentum Epistolce St. Pauli ad Romanos,* c. xvi.) Eusebius Pamphilus, if we can credit the quotation of him by a very untrustworthy author, Simeon Metaphrastes, states St. Peter to have been in Britain as well as Rome. — (*Metaphrastes ad 29 Junii.*) The vision to which St. Peter refers, 2 Pet. i. 14, "Knowing that shortly I must put off this my tabernacle, even as our Lord Jesus Christ hath shewed me," is said to have appeared to him in Britain on the spot where once stood the British Church of Lambedr (St. Peter), and now stands the Abbey of St. Peter's, Westminster. Lambeth may be a corruption of Lambedr. But this question lies between Roman Catholic authors and their own Church, which will scarcely put the seal of its infallibility on a position that places the British Church on its own special appropriated Rock.

[9] Bede was a very earnest adherent of the novel papal Church, introduced A.D. 596, by Augustine into Britain, but the honesty and simplicity of his character has rendered his history in many respects a very inconvenient and obnoxious record to the said Church. What became of the remains of St. Peter and St. Paul? At Rome they still pretend to exhibit them, but Bede — and it must be remembered he is a canonized saint in the Roman calendar — expressly states that the remains of the bodies of the apostles Peter and Paul, the martyrs St. Lawrence, St. John, St. Gregory, and St. Pancras, were, at the solicitation of King Oswy to Pope Vitalian, removed from Rome to England, and deposited at Canterbury A.D. 656, Pope Vitalian's letter to Oswy being extant. (Bedoe hist., lib. iii. c. 29.) Their remains, then, if any, repose in British soil.

Conclusion

From the preceding investigation ensue the following conclusions: —

1. Before Christianity originated in Judaea, there had existed from the remotest period in Britain a religion known as the Druidic, of which the two leading doctrines were identical with those of Christianity, viz., the immortality of the soul and vicarious atonement.

2. That this identity pointed out Britain as of all Gentile countries the one best prepared for the reception of Christianity.

3. That the only religions persecuted by the Roman government were the Druidic and the Christian.

4. That this common persecution by the great military empire with which Britain was engaged in incessant hostilities from A.D. 43 to A.D. 118, materially aided in predisposing the British mind in favour of Christianity.

5. That Britain, being the only free state of Europe, was the only country which afforded a secure asylum to the Christians persecuted by the Roman government.

6. That a current of Christianity flowed into Britain from the East contemporaneously with the first dispersion of the Church at Jerusalem, A.D. 35 — 38.

7. That the first planters of the Gospel in Britain never were in Rome at all, but came hither from the mother Church at Jerusalem.

8. That these first planters were Joseph of Arimathaea and his associates, who settled under the protection of the British king Arviragus, in the Isle of Avàlon, Glastonbury — one of the Druidic cors of Somerset.

9. That among the earliest converts of Joseph and his fraternity were Gladys (Pomponia Graecina) the sister, Gladys or Claudia, and Eurgain, the daughters, and Linus the son of Caractacus, prince of Siluria, and military dictator of the national forces against the Romans.

10. That the second planter of the word was Simon Zelotes the apostle, who was martyred and buried in the Roman province, probably near Caistor, in Lincolnshire.

11. That the third planter was Aristobulus, one of the seventy, brother of St. Barnabas and father-in-law of St. Peter; commissioned first bishop of Britain by St. Paul, and consecrated by St. Barnabas, the two apostles to the Gentiles. That Aristobulus was engaged in his mission in Britain when St. Paul wrote his Epistle to the Romans, some years before his first visit, or the visit of any other apostle, to Rome.

12. That Pudens, the husband of Claudia, Claudia herself, the sister Eurgain, her brother Linus, and aunt Pomponia, being converted prior to St. Paul's visit to Rome, the rest of the British royal family, Bran, Caractacus, Cyllinus and Cynon, were converted and baptized by St. Paul himself during his detention in that city preceding his first trial. That the palace of Pudens and Claudia was the home of St. Paul and the other apostles; that their four children, Timotheus, Novatus, Pudentiana and Praxedes, were instructed in the faith by St. Paul; and that Linus, the brother of Claudia and second son of Caractacus, was appointed by the same apostle first bishop of the Church of Rome, such Church meeting at that time, and till the reign of Constantine, in the aforesaid palace, called indifferently "Domus Pudentis, Palatium Britannicum, Domus Apostolorum, Titulus, Pastor, St. Pudentiana."

13. That after the return of Caractacus to Siluria, St. Paul himself, following the footsteps of his bishop and forerunner, Aristobulus, visited Britain, and confirmed the British Churches in the faith.

14. That the last days of St. Paul, preceding his martyrdom at Rome, were attended by Pudens, Claudia, Linus, Eubulus, whose salutations he sends in his dying charge to Timothy, and that his remains were interred by them in their family sepulchre.

15. That the foundations of the British Church were Apostolical, being coeval, within a few years, with those of the Pentecostal Church in Jerusalem — preceding those of the primitive Church of Rome, so far as they were laid by either an apostle or apostolic bishop, by seven years — preceding the arrival of St. Peter at Rome, as fixed by the great majority of Roman Catholic historians (thirteenth year of Nero), by thirty years — preceding the first arrival of the papal Church of Rome in Britain, under Augustine, by 456 years.

16. That the British Church has from its origin been a royal one; the royal family of ancient Britain — of whom our present sovereign is, through the Tudors, the lineal blood representative — being 1. the first British converts to Christianity; 2. the founders of the first Christian institutions in Britain; 3. the chief instruments, in the second century, in the establishment of Christianity as the state religion; and in the fourth century, in the persons of Helen and Constantine the Great, the chief instrument in the abolition of Paganism, and the substitution, in its place, of Christianity over the whole Roman Empire.

17. That the spiritual or ecclesiastical head of the British Church was always a Briton, resident in Britain, amenable to British laws, and British laws only, and having no superior in the Church but Christ.

18. That whatever may be the religious advantages or disadvantages of the union of the ecclesiastical and civil governments in the person of the Sovereign, such union has been, from the first colonization of our Island,

first in Druidic and then in Christian times, the native British, as opposed to the foreign papal — and, in later times, dissenting — principle of their separation.

www.ingramcontent.com/pod-product-compliance
Lightning Source LLC
Chambersburg PA
CBHW031415040426
42444CB00005B/584